BOILING OFF
MAPLE SUGARING IN MAINE

JOHN HODGKINS

CAMDEN, MAINE

Down East Books

Published by Down East Books
An imprint of Globe Pequot
Trade division of The Rowman & Littlefield Publishing Group, Inc.
4501 Forbes Blvd., Ste. 200
Lanham, MD 20706
www.rowman.com
www.downeastbooks.com

Distributed by NATIONAL BOOK NETWORK

ISBN 978-1-60893-684-7 (paper)
ISBN 978-1-60893-685-4 (e-book)

∞™ The paper used in this publication meets the minimum requirements of American National Standard for Information Sciences—Permanence of Paper for Printed Library Materials, ANSI/NISO Z39.48-1992.

Dedicated to
Beth, who spent fifty-some years by my side
seeking maple syrup excellence.

CONTENTS

CONTENTS

INTRODUCTION

NEAR THE END OF SUGARING SEASON 2013, THE MAINE MAPLE PRO-
ducers Association (MMPA) hosted a pancake breakfast in Skowhegan.
A hundred or so Maine sugarmakers, spouses, and families gathered at the
Tewksbury Building on Island Avenue to observe the thirtieth anniversary
of Maine's annual open saphouse, Maine Maple Sunday®, and to recognize its founders, the 1983 MMPA Board of Directors. Six of the nine-
member 1983 board attended the breakfast. Thirty years had passed since
we had met in Skowhegan and famously designated the fourth Sunday
in March as Maine Maple Sunday®.

Following the pancakes, Lyle Merrifield, president of MMPA, introduced the six, presented each of us with an engraved wooden plaque as
a tribute to our historic decision in 1983, and allotted each of us two
minutes for remarks. Arnold Luce, 1983 president of MMPA, whose
presidency was characterized by his emphasis on marketing Maine maple
syrup, spoke first. Luce sugared in Anson then, on the site where he
and his ancestry had sugared since 1884; before that in New Vineyard,
producing sugar and syrup as far back as 1795. Luce recalled the 1983
board meeting and, when presented a plaque, used his two minutes giving credit to Ted Greene for naming the celebratory day Maine Maple
Sunday. Greene, whose ancestry had sugared on the rocky outcrops of
Mac's Corner in East Sebago since the nineteenth century, recalled what
he could remember of the 1983 meeting and then denied that it had been
him who had named Maine Maple Sunday. He passed the naming honor
on to me. During my two minutes, I declined the recognition, citing that
it was my first board meeting and I was focused instead on learning what
the bylaws actually required of a board member. I returned the honor to

Greene, he being the most logical candidate, secretary of MMPA and all. I did, however, in a rare moment of insanity at the lectern, allege that my fifty years of sugaring in Temple made me the dean of active sugarmakers in Maine. John Steeves was next to receive a plaque.

Steeves told the audience that five generations of the Steeves family had sugared, the most recent site in Skowhegan, where he and his son Jeremy have produced maple syrup from thirteen thousand tapholes since 1968. Steeves also recalled that he hosted the unforgettable 1983 board meeting in his parlor in Skowhegan and served the board cookies during the historic discussion of naming the new festivity. He then disclosed that 2013 was his seventy-second year of producing maple syrup.

Bob Smith, the next recipient of a plaque, started sugaring in 1964 with a roadside sap route through five towns surrounding Skowhegan; he collected sap with a Jeep and a U-Haul trailer and boiled off the syrup in a Silver Street sugarhouse downtown. Smith, three terms as MMPA president as part of his resume, is the only Maine sugarmaker to have been inducted into the Maple Hall of Fame at the American Maple Museum in Croghan, New York. It happened in 2001, when Smith's resume included also tapping twelve thousand sugar maples in Township 7 Range 19, more than one hundred miles north of Skowhegan. Peter Tracy was next at the dais. Tracy sugared at Maple Hill Farm on Titcomb Hill in Farmington, the descendent farm of Stephen Titcomb, Maine's first maple producer, and was the keeper of Titcomb's old kettle. Tracy graciously admitted that he had nothing to do with naming Maine Maple Sunday.

The six honorees represented more than eight hundred years of Maine sugaring experience, enough, I thought, to warrant a book on Maine sugaring. I also thought a book necessary. Except for *The Maple Sugar Book* by Helen and Scott Nearing of their sugaring experiences in Vermont, little has been written of actual sugaring practices by production sugarmakers, no less a book, one that would fit in a bookcase and not necessarily need a coffee table to support it. I've written two books on historical America, I mused: one from the World War II period and the other from the town ball era, both successful. I've produced maple syrup commercially for fifty-two years; I have memories; I can tell stories; I can relate personal know-how—or don't-know-how—and show readers where I found snags and where I didn't. I have records too, disorganized and scattered, but records nevertheless. I know the scale of Maine maple sugaring, that it's big business, that producers exist in Maine with as many as eighty thousand tapholes; yet the less-than-two-thousand-taphole crowd, where I reside, dominates the culture. I can do it. I can take on such a project, I think.

I was twenty-nine years old when I started sugaring in 1964. I didn't know a thing about it. Didn't need to, I thought. But despite the unknown in front of me, I joined Brud and Bill, two cousins, and straight away tapped three thousand sugar maples deep in the woods behind Temple, Maine. We called ourselves Jackson Mountain Maple Farm. That was 1964. In 1965, I wanted to stop. Sugaring was too much, I thought. Too intense. I knew too little of how to do it well. One day a friend hiked up the hill to see what I was doing. We walked into the unkempt forest where my buckets were hanging, and looked down onto the saphouse below. "I have a vision," I told him, as though what I saw bore little resemblance to sugaring as I envisioned it. I seemed destined, however. Some force, perhaps a natural aversion to mediocrity or bull-headedness or the pleasant sense of being in the natural world, propelled me onward. Whatever, I couldn't stop. Not in 1965—not ever.

Boiling Off is the story of making maple syrup commercially in Temple, Maine, for fifty-some years. And weaved into the story of Jackson Mountain Maple Farm is the history of Maine sugaring, beginning in Farmington in 1781 when Stephen Titcomb boiled off the first official pure Maine maple syrup in a cast iron kettle. *Boiling Off* tracks the evolution of sugaring technology from Titcomb's kettle to the Leader company's MAXflue pan and heat exchanger; sap-gathering techniques from buckets and oxen-drawn drays to Warren Voter's introduction of plastic tubing; and records Maine maple syrup production, from 8,000 gallons produced by Maine licensed producers in 1985 to 709,000 gallons in 2017. The story describes the subtleties of syrup flavor, how it's properly graded, and the art of making award-winning Maine maple syrup. And it reveals who the producers of Maine maple syrup are, where it is harvested, and how L.L. Bean came to first stock it on their shelves. And it recounts the trials we suffered at Jackson Mountain Maple Farm.

For fifty years, Jackson Mountain Maple Farm endured a continuous challenge of sugaring obstacles that I had no knowledge of how to overcome: the devastating effect of unleashed bacteria; the inherent inefficiency of sap collection; the risks of not balancing the depth of sap in the boiling pans with syrup production at the draw; the difficulty configuring plastic pipeline networks for maximum sap yield; and the alluring pursuit of flavor are just some of the difficulties I faced. But the pleasure that came from the sweet syrup when it was done right: its flavor, its grade—color—and its popularity with customers who smiled at its pure maple taste, countered a lot of the suffering. "Yours is the best-tasting maple syrup I've *ever* tasted," a customer once told me. "The best syrup of all," another wrote. I don't regret the suffering.

During the time of the writing, which took up as many as six long years, the Maine Department of Agriculture issued approximately 450 licenses annually to produce pure Maine maple syrup. I talked with many of those producers, some for only a single question, others a lengthy conversation. All were quick to offer their help. Bob Smith, for example, filled out a full-page questionnaire for me. Arnold Luce took me through his family's sugaring history. John Graham and Miguel Ibarguen at Bowley Brook swapped emails with me for most of a sugaring season. Peter Tracy at Maple Hill Farm on Titcomb Hill in Farmington furnished historic information on the coming of Stephen Titcomb to Titcomb Hill. For all of this, and more, I am indebted.

I am also grateful to others for allowing me to use their material: Bob Smith for a 1930s map of the Maine Maple Sugar District; Earle Mitchell in Bowdoin for interview notes he accumulated while producing sugarmaker profiles for *Maple News*; Jo Josephson, a Temple neighbor whom I also referred to occasionally as my publicist, for use of an occasional photograph taken in the saphouse; Lyle Merrifield, MMPA president, and Kathryn Hopkins, MMPA member and maple educator, for their generous contributions; Walter Gooley for use of photos taken by him while he was Maine's maple syrup specialist; Earle Mitchell again for permission to use a sketch or two of his; Chandler Woodcock, Maine poet, for "Jackson Mountain," a poem that reveals all. Without you all there is no story. Many thanks.

Chapter One

1781 PLANTATION NUMBER ONE

I FIRST MADE MAPLE SYRUP—SUGARED—IN 1944. I KNEW LITTLE about sugaring then, but Pa was away at war and the government had rationed sugar. Ma, left behind in tiny Temple, Maine, pretty much on her own, needed some sweetener, and she showed me how to use Pa's bit brace and bit. Though only nine years old and not handy with tools, I saw an opportunity to help out on the home front.

I went to work. With the bit and brace I drilled a half-dozen holes in the sugar maples that lined the road in front of our house, inserted metal spiles, as they were called then, and hung tin cans to catch the sap that dripped over the end of the spiles. As the cans filled, I took the sap to Ma and she steamed it down on the kitchen cook stove into a thick, murky liquid and put it in a jar. I don't recall us producing any sugar—nor do I recall the wallpaper falling from the kitchen walls as such stories are usually told—but Ma did drizzle some of the life-giving sweet liquid onto our breakfast pancakes a few days later. I felt a part of the cause; I had a role in the war; I was a soldier, too. With the coming of summer though, I put away the bit and brace and pails and spiles, and Ma trained me to use Pa's lawnmower. Later, while the war still raged, I raked scatterings in Uncle Sheriden's haying crew. Twenty years would pass before I produced any more maple syrup.

The first pure maple syrup made in Maine, it's widely held, came from Stephen Titcomb's place on the bank of Sandy River in what was known then as Plantation Number One, now Farmington Falls. Titcomb is claimed to have produced syrup there in 1781.

In December 1780, so the story goes, nine years before George Washington was inaugurated president of the United States, Titcomb and his family left Topsham, Maine, in a two-ox wagon—some say a sled—and headed north. Stowed in the small wooden buckboard were the necessaries of homesteading: a larder of dried and salted food; overcoats, snowshoes, and furniture; a bed, a mirror, and a wooden keg. Seed corn was packed under the seat. Two cows and a few sheep trotted alongside. The driver, Stephen Titcomb, a forward-looking man some thirty years old, herded the oxen and animals northerly sixty miles distant toward Plantation Number One and a piece of land alongside Sandy River. In 1776 Titcomb had come to Plantation One via the Kennebec River with partners Robert Gower and others, cleared land, and staked out a lot. In subsequent years he built a cabin, tilled land, and made maple syrup. This year—1780—he was coming to stay.

Four passengers accompanied Titcomb: wife, Elizabeth, snuggled one-month-old Hannah, and two sons, two-year-old Henry and four-year-old Joseph, who watched over the wagon's sideboards and examined the earth as it passed beneath them.

Their first year in Plantation One, it's said, the boys passed their days playing on the river's sandy beaches. One day Joseph dug up an old cast iron kettle buried in the sand, a kettle thought to have been left behind by Abenaki Indians who had encamped there some time previously. Titcomb, perhaps Maine's first sugarmaker, saved the kettle and put it to work in the spring boiling off maple syrup and sugar.

In 1808 Joseph Titcomb, now thirty years old, married and built a house in Farmington village. In 1820, unwilling to bring up his family amid the temptations of village life, he moved one mile to Titcomb Hill. In March 1820, so the story goes, he and his father, Stephen, using the old kettle he'd found buried in Sandy River years ago, boiled off what is declared to be the first batch of pure maple syrup made in the state of Maine. A hundred years later, Nellie Titcomb Williams, a fourth—or fifth, or sixth—generation descendent of Stephen, and her husband, Charles, produced syrup on the same Titcomb Hill farm, known then as Maple Hill Fruit Farm. The old kettle hung in Nellie's saphouse then, a tribute to sugaring history. In 1971, Albion and Donna Tracy acquired Maple Hill Fruit Farm—the kettle as well—and renamed it Maple Hill Farm. The Tracys continue even now to produce pure Maine maple syrup at Maple Hill Farm, displaying the old kettle every sugaring season on Maine Maple Sunday.

The use of an iron kettle to boil sap, according to Helen and Scott Nearing in *The Maple Sugar Book*, was the first innovation in the Indian way of sugaring. The Indian way, as the Nearings described it, was to hollow out troughs from downed tree trunks, place sap in the troughs, and insert heated stones hot enough to cause the sap to boil—or steam. This method was used for making sugar until the arrival in North America of European explorers and fur traders. Not until the European traders brought metal to North America, perhaps early in the eighteenth century, was the iron kettle used to make maple syrup and sugar. Kettles and pots, though popular for boiling off syrup or sugar, produced syrup that usually tasted dark and strong due to the lengthy boiling time and the cook's need to keep adding sap to the boiling kettle.

The Natives, though likely the first to make sugar from the sap of the sugar maple tree, are not so likely the discoverers of the sweetness in sugar maple sap. Yes, the Natives made and used maple sugar before anyone. They just didn't *discover* it. The sweetness in maple sap was shown to them, passed down you might say. The American red squirrel, *Tamiasciurus hudsonicus*, the chatterer, it's said, discovered the sweetness in maple sap. The American red squirrel dates from the Ice Age, ten thousand years ago, and is known, as many producers have observed, to chew into maple trees in the spring and drink the sap. The American red squirrel also gnaws into the bottom side of a sugar maple limb, lets the sap ooze out onto a branch, and returns later, after sunlight has evaporated moisture out of the sap, and devours the residue. The American red squirrel is the only rodent observed to harvest and evaporate maple sap. The early Natives likely made the same observation.

9

CHAPTER TWO

SUGAR MAPLES

IN 1963, NEARLY 150 YEARS AFTER STEPHEN TITCOMB BOILED OFF THE first pure Maine maple syrup in Farmington, and twenty years since my first attempt at sugaring on the front lawn in Temple, circumstance tempts me again to the sugar maple.

Brud Hodgkins, a nineteen-year-old cousin studying civil engineering at the university, comes to see me. He's been running a vibrant sap-gathering business in Temple village for several years, he tells me, wheedling his young friends in town to tap sugar maples and sell him the sap. He pays them eight cents a gallon, and transports the sap five miles to Warren Voter's sugar shack on Voter Hill in West Farmington. For every thirty gallons of sap Brud delivers, Voter makes a gallon of syrup. He pays for the sap with half the syrup, puts it in a container Brud brings with him, and puts the other half into his own lithographed tin cans. The value of Voter's gallon of syrup in 1963 is $5. Brud's half is worth $2.50. He paid, I calculate, $2.40 to the kids in Temple for the sap, and has received $2.50 from Voter in syrup. Brud says he doesn't like Voter's deal. "I want it all," he tells me. "You and I and Bill—Brud's fourteen-year-old brother—could tap our own trees, boil it off ourselves, and have it all."

I don't know, of course. I'm twenty-eight years old, unmarried, roaming around Maine in quest of a civil engineering career. I don't know anything about the commercial production of maple syrup. I've never seen maple sap gathered, never seen maple sap boiled off into maple syrup in a set of commercial evaporator pans, never sold any maple syrup—or purchased any. My experience is limited to 1944 and the kitchen stove.

We talk. Brud's plan for producing syrup is not complicated. Assertive, sure of his ground—businessman, too—he relates his plan to me while he doodles in a small notebook full of numbers and lists. I listen to him. "Borrow the money," he says. "Put out two, maybe three thousand buckets." He says we'll hire someone to collect and deliver the sap to a sapshack some local carpenter will build for us and sell the syrup ourselves, seven hundred gallons a year, he estimates. "Should get $6,000 for it," he says.

The plan does not excite me. Too many loose ends. Too much reliance on characters yet unknown to me: a carpenter, a gathering crew, Voter and his syrup-making know-how, and a source of money. I feel, on the other hand, a certain excitement, a challenge. They need me. I can be part of it. We talk late into the night, two tired voices sitting in the dark. "Why?" I ask him. "Why maple syrup?"

"'Cause I'm sick and tired of buying sap someone else gathers and taking it over to Warren's in milk cans," he says again, "an' then only getting half the syrup. If I boil it off myself, I can have it all." He hesitates and lets me absorb what he has said. Then he goes on, "I think we all together, you and I and Bill, we could set up an operation and boil it off right here in Temple."

I know enough to know that we will need more than a paltry few sugar maples on someone's lawn. I know, too, that neither of us has any money. "So where's the money come from?" I ask.

"The bank," he answers.

Now I know why I'm in this conversation. I'm not troubled that I'll be the one going to the bank, however. Perhaps I'll learn something about sugaring. "And the trees?" I query. "Where are the trees?"

"They're up in Hellgren's woodlot on Day Mountain Road, three thousand of 'em."

In 1963, Maine, according to the United States Department of Agriculture (USDA), is 90 percent forested, the most heavily forested state in America. The same was true when the Pilgrims arrived in 1620.

During the period 1775 to 1875, however, seven million acres of Maine's forests—40 percent—were cleared for settlement. Pioneers came into Maine beginning in the mid-1700s, acquired land, cleared the forest, built farmsteads in the hills, and put the land into production, agriculture, dairy, and livestock. One hundred years later, farming the Maine hills, as well as hills in New Hampshire and Vermont, had failed. A living could not be sustained. Farms were abandoned, agricultural land went fallow, and the forest came back. By 1965 or so, according to the USDA's *The Forests of Maine*, the cleared land had regrown, and Maine's forest had reached its pre-1775 forested condition, 90 percent of the state. The Maine Forest Service classified much of it, more than seven million acres of deciduous trees, as northern mixed hardwood, predominately sugar maple (*Acer saccharum*), American beech, and yellow birch—sugar maple is the most prevalent.

Sugar maple trees grow abundantly in about two-thirds of the state, mostly on the high plateaus and low mountains that envelop the western and northwestern forests behind the coastal plain, from some six hundred or more feet above sea level to as high as two thousand feet, in hilly and well-drained soil where winter is cold and still and spring temperatures pulsate through March and April toward summer. In 1951, the USDA Agricultural Research Service reported fifty-three million sugar maples of greater than ten-inch diameter growing in Maine. At the same time, the USDA reported twenty-six million such trees growing in Vermont and twelve million in New Hampshire. It's likely that more maples of tapping size were growing in Maine in 1963 than ever. And they were easy to find.

Thirteen species of maple tree are known to produce sugary sap. Of the thirteen, sap from the sugar maple and black maple (*Acer nigrum*) contain the highest sugar concentrations, perhaps 4 percent sugar in trees with large, healthy crowns, enough to warrant commercial production of sugar and syrup. Sugar maple is a northeastern tree, plentiful in Maine. Black maple is Midwestern, its sugar content a dite less than that of sugar maple. Red maple (*Acer rubrum*)—called white maple, soft maple, or swamp maple by some Mainers—is also found in Maine, and many Maine producers tap it commercially. But red maple's sugar content is not quite up to that of the sugar maple. And it buds early in the spring, earlier than sugar maple. The post-buds sap of the red maple imparts a somewhat bitter off-taste to the resultant sugar or syrup and forces an earlier ending to the production of pancake-grade maple syrup. Maine producers, however, are cautious about tapping red maple, as the sap from a few red maples with swelled buds can foul an entire batch of sugar maple table-grade syrup with the buddy taste of red maple. Other eastern maple species—mountain maple, striped maple, big leaf maple, silver maple, and box elder—though containing slight levels of sugar, have no role in Maine sugaring. Maine's maple-sugaring crop comes from sugar maple and red maple.

Settled in 1796 by a group of ambitious and adventurous hill-farmers, Temple in 1963 is ideal for sugaring. The hilly town, all well above the qualifying six-hundred-foot sugaring elevation, has seen the rise and demise of hill-farming. The early agriculturists, finding it impossible to extract a living from Temple's barren hills, abandoned their farms in the mid-1800s, and in 1963, one hundred years or so later, the cleared land is producing trees again. Sugar maple, beech, and yellow birch forest—the dominant species of sugar maple—are filling in the high clearings. Sugar maple is abundant.

By 1964 Brud has done his prerequisite work. He has found a grove of mature sugar maples so deep into Temple's outback that it may actually be in neighboring Avon. The owner, Temple logger Vilio Hellgren, and his crew of cutters are poised to start another cutting cycle. Brud, however, sees potential in the stand of sugar maples and persuades Hellgren to let us assess its prospects for syrup making.

We like what we see. The land sits on both sides of an old settler road coming into Temple from Avon between two small hills. It pitches toward the south, giving us easterly, southerly, and westerly exposures to the sun, what will amount to a long day of sunshine. The grove contains a generous quantity of sugar maples more than ten inches in diameter measured at about the height that we will drill the tapholes. The land appears not to have been grazed in past years but has likely been thinned a bit—perhaps by the former hill-farmer Jackson—to improve the lot for sugar, taking out the beech, ash, and yellow birch for furniture and firewood, a common practice in the early days. The land is high, above 1,500 feet in elevation, well drained, and likely covered with prodigious amounts of snow throughout the spring months, keeping the tree roots cold and extending the maple syrup season. Brud, who seldom utters a negative thought, estimates three thousand tapholes are possible. We ignore the location, some two miles beyond the end of Temple's snow-plow route up Day Mountain Road, name ourselves Jackson Mountain Maple Farm, and go to Hellgren to negotiate an agreement to tap his trees.

A maple syrup producer has options to consider when acquiring sap from sources other than his own land. He will need tapping rights from the landowner. A lease is the most common practice of acquiring the rights, wherein a producer acquires the right to tap the trees and gather the sap himself. Another common option for acquiring sap from landowners is for the landowner to tap, gather, and deliver the sap either to the produc-er's saphouse or, in the case of the trees being off the road, to a convenient pickup point. Producers, in the case of when sap is being delivered by the landowner, require quick delivery to the saphouse to prevent sap from aging—meaning in most cases, of course, daily delivery. Another option for acquiring sap is for a syrup producer to lease a block of land. In this case the leased rights will include everything from sap to syrup; that is, building a sapshack, cutting firewood, constructing roads, and tapping and gathering sap. Determined sugarmakers will usually come up with a suitable option for obtaining sap.

The matter of payment for the sap, however, will provide another set of options. Historically, payment is usually made by one of two ways: per gallon of sap or per taphole. Payment is usually in money. In the occa-sional case of a small amount of sap, however, such as a neighbor's trees or a roadside route of multiple owners, payment is usually by a percentage of the syrup made from the sap. The amount of money paid per gallon for sap is determined from the sugar content. Producers will measure the volume and the Brix—percent by weight of sugar in the sap—when the sap is delivered and pay accordingly. Price will vary with the percentage of sugar. A higher Brix means more money—or more maple syrup. There are no fixed rules, however, for what is best. Producers and landowners are free to agree on whatever works. Brud, for example, paid his suppliers in Temple village eight cents per gallon for the sap he took to Warren Voter's sugar house. Voter paid Brud with syrup for the same sap.

Producers who lease large numbers of sugar maples and acquire large volumes of sap prefer to pay a fee per taphole leased to avoid cumbersome measurements—or inexact estimates—of volume and Brix. Landowners will often see this method as less risky and prefer a fee per taphole. Producers will see it as less risky also, though they are aware of the possibility of a bad season and may factor that into their negotiations. This type of lease is usually renewed periodically to adjust for change in conditions—or costs. As we approach Hellgren, we face these various leasing options.

Our proposal to Hellgren is to lease his land, about one hundred acres, and the maple trees there for the purpose of producing maple syrup and maple sugar. We intend to build a saphouse, tap and collect sap from the surrounding sugar maple groves, and boil it off on the site; that is, a saphouse. Firewood will come from off-site. "And it will likely be mud season," Brud explains to Hellgren. "We will need you and your logging crew to gather the sap."

Hellgren's logging crew comprises two woodchoppers, Eddie Fontaine and Mike Bergeron. Fontaine, a Quebecker, hopped off a southbound freight train at age sixteen in northern Vermont and worked his way easterly across New England logging and tending to hill farming for folks who needed him. He showed up in Temple twenty years later, 1938, and became the local handy man. He built steps, tuned engines, chopped wood, tended cows, carved ax handles, lined wells, grafted apple trees, slaughtered pigs, and whatever else Temple folks needed done. A journalist once described Fontaine as "an expert at several obsolete skills."

He also knew maple sugaring; he learned it in Quebec as a teenager. In 1964 he operates a chain saw in Hellgren's logging crew.

Mike Bergeron, on the other hand, is working his first job. A high school graduate less than a year ago, he works logging with Hellgren and Fontaine while he ponders what will be next. Strong, bright, conscientious, Bergeron is a hard worker and we like him—Hellgren does too—but sugaring season is mud season in Temple, and logging is often stymied by impassable roads for five or six weeks. I suspect Bergeron sees a personal financial benefit in sugaring, a substitute income for otherwise idle time. I suspect he looks forward to the extra money. We look forward to having Bergeron on the crew.

Hellgren, best defined perhaps as a gentleman logger, is a hard worker too. Born in Temple the son of immigrant Finns, he grew up here during the Great Depression, left school to work in the woods, and has scraped out a hardscrabble life with hard work and honesty. He soldiered in World War II, played center field for the postwar Temple Townies, and now, in addition to managing a successful logging business in Temple, serves his town as a public official. Folks in Temple trust him. An agreeable and principled person, he is willing to seal a deal with a handshake.

At our meeting he suggests to me that $125 per year will be sufficient for rights to tap his trees. I propose that the lease remain in effect for ten years. He concurs. As promised, he's not interested in legalese. He doesn't need the agreement witnessed and endorsed by out-of-town lawyers and other strangers, either. He and I both know, however, that land agreements require signatures.

The agreement is for tapping rights. It includes provisions for access to all parts of the land, construction of facilities, tapping rights to all sugar maple trees on the land, and that the lessor (Hellgren) will retain the right to continue lumbering on the land exclusive of cutting maple trees. The agreement also cites the annual fee of $125 payable to the lessor, and that the lease shall remain in effect for ten years. When it's time to sign, Hellgren reiterates to me his intention that no legal issues arise out of our sugaring his land, that this agreement, though we will sign it, is but a handshake, and that we'll work out any problems together. I agree and shake his hand.

But Hellgren isn't done. He asks me whether, during the ten years of the agreement, he can be allowed to "cut a few of the straight and best maple now and again." We discuss his request a bit, and then I write a provision on the bottom of the agreement stating such. Now time comes to sign. We are paying the equivalent of five cents per taphole for potentially ten gallons of sap, realistically five gallons, possibly three. More than fair, I think, and I sign. Hellgren signs. It's January 27, 1964. We have trees.

February comes. Brud says we will start tapping trees in about a month. Much work is left to do. We need a saphouse, equipment, and more time.

A LIST OF NECESSARIES

It's January 1964. Jackson Mountain Maple Farm has two months to the first sap run. We are at zero. We have nothing save a lease with Hellgren. Brud shows me what he describes as a list of necessaries, the essentials of maple syrup production. The list is long, anchored by a five-foot-wide-by-fourteen-foot-long Leader Special set of evaporator pans, the boiling rig that will turn our sap into maple syrup.

The Leader Special evaporator, an updated version of the Leader Regular, was introduced to the maple world by the Leader Evaporator Company, the nation's premier maple equipment manufacturer, in 1905. It was said in 1963 to be the most popular evaporator style sold. The evaporator consists of an arrangement of three tin pans: an eight-foot flue pan and a six-foot front (flat) pan that sit on a fourteen-foot arch, and a heater pan, or warming pan, that perches crosswise on the top of the front end of the flue pan. This Leader Special arrangement comprises 350 square feet of English-tin surface exposed to the fire.

The heater pan is heated by the escaping steam. It will, Leader says, heat the cold sap coming from the storage tank to near 100°F before it enters the flues. But it's the flue pan where the work will be done. In the flue pan, sap boils and foams and riles and thrashes its way through two sets of flues, calmed a bit on its way by a drop or two of butter or salt pork, and then thickened a dite by the flogging it receives in the flues. Then it comes to the flat front pan where it's finished off. The Leader company says the rig will boil off 250 gallons of sap in an hour, enough to make about six gallons of maple syrup from 2 percent sap. We think it the right size for our Jackson Mountain endeavor. We order a big Leader Special.

Before the Leader Special came along in 1905, syrup in Maine was made in a variety of boiling vessels. First, of course, the Natives and settlers boiled sap in an iron kettle similar to what Stephen Titcomb used in the late 1700s in Farmington, a single kettle hung over an open fire. Later, with the coming of the nineteenth century, the kettle evolved into larger vessels—cauldrons—in multiples of two or three or four strung on a rod across an open fire. Still later, the kettles nestled into an enclosed arch of stone or brick over the fire. Boiling sap in these deep kettles, however, produced sugar—or syrup—dark in color and sometimes scorched and bitter in taste. Kettles also were inefficient. Sap boiled slowly—long, deep, and often untended. Left to smolder, kettles produced noticeably strong—even rank—tasting syrup.

At about the time of the Civil War and the coming of sheet metal, maple producers started fashioning flat-bottomed pans. The flat-bottomed pan, which presented considerably more hot surface to the sap than the kettle and allowed for shallow and quick boiling, made better tasting sugar and syrup—and made it faster. Henceforth, maple producers replaced kettles with flat pans. The very first flat-bottomed pans likely came from producers who tacked sheet iron to side and end panels made of wood, similar to an abandoned flat-bottomed pan I saw once in an old rough-boarded sorghum shack in Mississippi, where cane syrup producers used the same boiling arrangements to produce sorghum as we do maple syrup. The metal bottom protected the eight-inch wooden sides from burning; the high sides prevented smoke from roiling into the pan; and the wooden sides and end panels eliminated the need for bending and welding the metal. Eventually, of course, tin replaced the wooden sides and panels.

Flat pans probably reached Maine around 1880. Nellie Titcomb Williams, sugaring on Titcomb Hill in Farmington fifty years after the Civil War, described her flat pan as "a large bakersheet, three or four feet long by two feet wide and only a few inches deep." It was this bakersheet shape that offered flat pans advantages over kettles. And the high sides presumably kept the smoke from fouling the taste of maple syrup.

Innovators soon fashioned multiple flat-bottomed pans into a "continuous-flow evaporator," an arrangement that allowed the boiling sap to flow from pan to pan and finally to the end (front) pan, where the syrup reached its requisite boiling temperature and finished off. Continuous-flow evaporators reduced the boiling time even more and improved the clarity and taste of syrup as well. These multiple-pan evaporators, however, as much as producers lauded over them, were only precursors to an evaporator that incorporated the so-called flue pan. The flue pan, perhaps the most significant improvement in the history of maple sap evaporation until the arrival of reverse osmosis nearly a hundred years later, appeared in 1890.

At Jackson Mountain Maple Farm, our selection of a big Leader Special evaporator prompts a caboodle of other needs. Brud's list of necessaries is a very long list, a list about the same length as a winter night in Maine, so to speak, and includes an iron arch and firebox for the big Leader Special to sit on, complete with fifteen feet of nineteen-inch diameter smoke-stack fabricated to fit the rear of the arch and extend through the roof above. And there's more. Two storage tanks, two gathering tanks, a four-cone filter tank, an electrified thermo-valve system said to draw off the syrup at the specified temperature automatically, piping, a sap hydrome-ter, a hydrotherm, two sets of wool filters for the four-cone filter tank, a gasoline-powered tapping machine, 2,500 malleable iron spouts, several seven-sixteenths-inch drill bits, a pellet gun, and three thousand galva-nized, fifteen-quart sap buckets previously used by a New York maple producer. Brud estimates the cost to be $5,000. My role in this maple syrup venture, heretofore a bit indeterminate, now comes into focus. It's not the syruping skills I acquired in 1944, or my engineering training at the university, or my ability to read a contract that has brought me here. "Place the order," I tell teenager Brud. "I'll go to the bank."

The New York sap buckets—I learn later that they came to Leader from a progressive New York, or perhaps Vermont, producer who had exchanged them for a network of plastic tubing—were a welcome discovery. I come back from the bank with $6,000, and I don't want to go again. Priced at 40 percent of the price new, the bucket discount keeps us within our meager budget. The bucket deal alone reduces our equipment outlay by more than $2,000, and now we have a surplus of money. Perhaps we can pay the sap crew, acquire fuel, and buy syrup cans before we need revenue from the much anticipated seven hundred gallons of syrup we'll produce—or so I think we will.

The pellet gun, a small, orange, plastic cylindrical container with a hollow gun barrel on one end and a plunger on the other, is used to inject a pellet into a taphole. The pellet, a paraformaldehyde sanitizing tablet, Warren Voter tells us, will keep the taphole fresh and running freely throughout the entire season, and prevent the presence of mischievous bacteria, the invisible curse of sap producers, from sealing the taphole's sidewalls and blocking the sap flow. Brud adds three thousand pellets to the list. When tapping time comes, we will insert one, perhaps two if the gun accidentally jams or misfires, into each taphole.

Prior to the coming of the paraformaldehyde tablet in 1962, producers took time in midseason to ream their holes, freshen the inside walls, with another pass of a bit or reaming tool. It was laborious and onerous work, but the risk of not doing so, as much as a third of the season lost, would cost even more. A producer who put in four thousand taps, such as Richard Eaton in East Corinth did in 1946, could expect to lose well over three hundred gallons of maple syrup in a normal season should he not renew the holes midway, an expensive—in 1970 about $2,500 in syrup lost—consequence of avoiding what had become essential work. In a 1946 letter to Kenneth Cooper, a maple producer in Buckfield, Eaton wailed, "One man here did just right and he made as much syrup from three thousand as I did from four thousand!"

It comes time in February for Jackson Mountain Maple Farm to have a saphouse. In our case, a saphouse will not only be for processing sap into maple syrup protected from the weather. Space will be provided for storage of buckets, equipment such as gathering pails and sap pumps, empty containers, and sundry tools and supplies. The sap storage tanks will be in an ell off the side of the saphouse and close to the road. A filtering tank will occupy space handy to the evaporator. And we will need space to eat meals—and possibly sleep.

Brud sketches a plan and delivers it to Dick Blodgett, a local handyman who specializes in cabinet making. "We need a sturdy saphouse," Brud tells him. "No shack for us." We locate the sapshack in the midst of our bush, somewhere in the shallow pass between our two nubbles of sugar maples. Blodgett will build it from the ground up with space to house boiling pans, a filtering station, countertops, and the storage tanks in the ell. He protects the piece of roof surrounding the stack with a piece of tin fashioned to keep the rain out and intended to also keep the stack's heat away from the wooden roof. "Do we need a floor?" I ask.

"No, no time for a floor. We don't need a floor. We'll level the arch on concrete blocks, and throw a few boards on the dirt for a floor." I'll need to wear boots up here, I think.

Blodgett frames the structure out of local timbers—two by twos, two by sixes, and structural pieces without dimensions—and faces the frame with boards and windows we salvage from the remnants of Temple's District Three schoolhouse, a homely and dilapidated structure from the last century two miles down Day Mountain Road that once housed a few hill-farm children and a volunteer schoolmarm during the school year. Most recently the schoolhouse has served as living space for Gust Walo, immigrant Finn and local laborer. The pieces of Walo's place, I feel, weather-beaten and broken as they are, give the sapshack authenticity, and place us in time some fifty years back, as well. And the cracks provide the ventilation Brud feels is necessary to maintain a robust fire under the pans. But is it sturdy? No. It's revisionist Temple history and, except for Walo's boards and the New York sap buckets, contemporary and modern. We furnish it with everything new.

The earliest sap gatherers, Natives and subsequent settlers, placed a wooden vessel—a trough hewed out of a tree trunk was popular—on the ground under a maple tree and caught sap in it. Beginning early in the nineteenth century and continuing until about the time of the Civil War, a wooden bucket fashioned from pine staves affixed to the tree served as a sap catchment for the growing maple sugar business. But wooden buckets and vessels proved unworthy. Sap soaked into the wood and soured, and the embedded residue, hard to remove, spoiled the sap and darkened the syrup. Following the Civil War, tin took over as the preferred material for manufacturing sap buckets. But tin was discovered to heat up considerably in sunlight, and it warmed the sap in the bucket, as well, and soon gave way to iron, followed by the popular fifteen-quart galvanized bucket and cover.

Maine syrup producers in 1964 commonly collect sap in fifteen-quart galvanized buckets. Though the three-gallon plastic sap bag, an inexpensive and reusable alternative that features a flap to protect the sap and keep it from spilling, are available, they are limited in the practical sense to suburban neighborhoods and rural front lawns. Sap bags are not popular with commercial producers. And plastic tubing, a gravity collection system that carries sap downhill without benefit of backbreaking labor, is also not fashionable among Maine producers in 1964. Popular in a few other states and emerging in still others—Warren Voter has tinkered with the idea—plastic tubing has not gained any more than a toehold in Maine. The sap collection technique of choice for Maine producers in 1964 comprises fifteen-quart buckets with suitable covers—all galvanized to resist rusting.

CHAPTER FOUR

TIME COMES TO TAP TREES

FEBRUARY COMES. THE DEAL WITH HELLGREN HAS BEEN SIGNED. THE essential equipment has been ordered from the Leader Evaporator Company in Burlington. Blodgett is constructing the saphouse. The *Old Farmer's Almanac*, the most popular astronomical and weather clairvoyant in America, predicts the first sap run will come on March 10, a bit more than a month from now. On February 3, word comes from Vermont that our equipment order is ready for pickup.

The following Saturday Brud, Bill, and I leave Temple at 4:00 a.m. in Hodgkins Store's red Chevy delivery truck filled with gas and food, and arrive at Leader's Battery Street plant in Burlington at noon. A Leader crew is waiting for us. It takes an hour to fill the truck with equipment and sundries. When we're done, half our order is still on the platform. We arrange for a watchman to let us in early Sunday morning and leave for Temple. Following a beef stew dinner and a short nap in Temple, we start again—for the second time today—a round trip across New England and back, a journey of more than four hundred miles. At 6:00 a.m. in Burlington, too early for the Leader crew to be up, we find an all-night Laundromat downtown and sleep on a tabletop for about an hour. At eight o'clock we take the truck to Leader's platform. At ten o'clock we leave for Temple, change drivers every two hours, and arrive home about six o'clock Sunday evening. Brud says he will look after the unloading. I go to bed. We now possess a collection of sugaring paraphernalia, though the pieces are scattered in sheds and barns all over Temple.

On March 4, a week before the much anticipated first sap run, time comes to tap trees. Brud breaks out our new three-quarter horsepower, gasoline-powered Comet drill, inserts a seven-sixteenths-inch bit, and starts drilling holes. He drills a tad more than two inches deep into each tree, usually on the southeastern side to catch the early morning sun. I follow Brud, fire a formaldehyde pellet into the hole with the plastic pellet pistol, and tap in a Warner malleable iron spout with a hammer. Bill hangs a bucket on the spout and slides a cover onto the bucket.

In 1964, metal spouts, whether manufactured from tin, cast iron, or malleable iron, are found on virtually all tapped sugar maples in Maine. Most brands—Warner, Soule, and Grimm the most popular—are similar in design. The Warner and Soule malleable iron spouts feature a tapered shank to seal a borehole seven-sixteenths of an inch in diameter, a channel for sap to flow through, a drip cap or bead, which the manufacturer claims to be a rain guard, a small eyelet, and a fixed hook for hanging the bucket. The eyelet, when furnished, permits a cover to be wired to the spout such that a bucket full of sap can be removed and dumped without removing and replacing the cover.

The Grimm spout, what Grimm calls the Ideal Spout, differs from the Warner and Soule in that the manufacturer, Grimm, forms it from a single piece of sheet steel and tapers it to permit use in boreholes of varying size. Coated to resist the formation of rust, the Ideal Spout is popular with backyard producers who usually tap only a few trees and use carpentry tools to bore the taphole and set the spout. Commercial producers, however, use malleable iron Warner and Soule spouts almost exclusively and have for fifty-some years.

Brud drills tapholes for five days. After 2,800 holes we run out of spouts. Too late to acquire more before the anticipated run, I whittle fifty out of sumac to fit another fifty holes, and then contact Leader about the missing two hundred. Bill hammers in nails and hangs the remaining buckets. We finish March 14, slowed by the whittling. The first sap run doesn't wait. It comes on March 8, two days ahead of schedule.

Before the onset of the twentieth century, back at the time of discovery when sugar was first produced from maple sap, Natives and settlers made spouts with a knife—or a hatchet. The first spouts—devices—for running sap into a vessel were wood chips or quills. Natives and settlers wedged a chip—or a quill—into the bottom end of a slanted slash in a tree cut with a hatchet or a knife. Sap would run down the slash, out to the end of the chip or quill, and drip into a vessel sitting next to the tree. Other devices may have been used as well—a reed, a piece of birch bark, or even the knife itself. Later, when the augured borehole came along, sugarmakers made spouts with a whittling knife and a wire. A three- or four-inch piece of sumac was popular. The whittler would, in turn, push out its soft center with a hot wire, whittle a channel on one end, and taper the other end to fit tight in any size hole. Still later, spouts were sawn from one-inch birch boards. A sawyer sliced the boards into one-inch by one-inch strips, cut the strips into six-inch pieces, tapered one end, and bore a one-quarter-inch-diameter hole through its entire six inches.

The first official metal sap spout appeared in 1860, patented by Eli Mosher of Flushing, Michigan. Fashioned by bending and grinding sheet metal into troughs, the cumbersome spouts in time gave way to cast iron, a somewhat brittle substance susceptible to breakage under the blows of a hammer. Soon, however, the malleable iron spout replaced the cast iron spout. Popular with most commercial sugarmakers in Maine, the malleable iron spout is cast as white iron and annealed—toughened—by heating into the malleable form. Malleable iron can be worked cold, stamped, bent, or coined to shape. It is highly ductile and virtually indestructible. Sugarmakers hammer malleable spouts at will without noticeable damage.

The first sap run comes to Jackson Mountain on March 8, 1964, a Sunday, two days earlier than *The Old Farmer's Almanac* had predicted. Hellgren comes with his dozer and drags a sled, a nine-barrel gathering tank mounted on its back, through the woods where the buckets—full and not so full of sap—hang waiting. He is followed by an entourage of volunteer sap gatherers—siblings, girlfriends, fraternity brothers, friends, and a group of local girl scouts—who dash through the woods tree to tree with truncated, inverted cone-shaped, fifteen-quart galvanized gathering pails. They pour the sap from the buckets into a gathering pail and, when full, dump the sap into the nine-barrel tank. When the tank fills, Hellgren drags the load to the saphouse where Brud drains the sap into one of our two storage tanks. Then back into the woods again.

It is classic sap gathering. The routine—a gathering pail, a vat or tub to dump the sap in, and a conveyance—comes out of necessity. It is the same as when the earliest gatherers lugged their sap in vessels from the trees to a central boiling kettle. We still, as the Natives and settlers did, gather sap from each tree separately and convey it to the fire in a vessel, in our case a bulldozer and an iron tub. All Maine commercial producers gather sap the same way, collect it tree to tree, dump it in a container, and convey it—somehow—to the fire. It is the only way. Absent any of the three items—tree, container, or conveyance—gathering and transporting sap to the fire is impossible.

Albion Tracy at Maple Hill Farm in Farmington uses oxen to pull a wooden tub on a dray; Earl Mitchell at Mitchell and Savage Maple Products in Bowdoin uses horses; Harold Gamage, a small producer in Litchfield, uses a sap yoke, suspending full gathering pails on his shoulders to carry the sap to the fire himself; Placide Couture, a start-up producer in North Jay, uses a galvanized gathering tank on a wooden sled dragged through the bush by a bulldozer, as we do on Jackson Mountain. Another first-year producer, Skowhegan forester Robert Smith, collects sap from a twenty-mile roadside sugarbush comprising the towns of Skowhegan, Norridgewock, Fairfield, Cornville, and Madison. He empties fifteen-quart buckets into gathering pails and dumps the sap into two seven-barrel gathering tanks on a U-Haul trailer pulled by an International Scout. He delivers his full tanks to a saphouse—central boiling point—in downtown Skowhegan.

Collecting and gathering sap in 1964 is not scientific. Nor was it in 1781 when the first maple syrup was made in the District of Maine. Stephen Titcomb used a gathering vessel, too; he filled it with sap and carried it to his fire and dumped it into the kettle. It's not science—it's work.

We gather the first-run sap until the buckets are empty. Perhaps something more than six hundred gallons, discounting sap that spills from the buckets, sloshes out of the gathering pails, and ricochets out of the tank from mishandling and from the bumpy route. The gathering pails and the tank are actually tapered internally in their manufacture to prevent accidental upward splash and the loss of sap. Occasionally the taper is effective and successfully blocks the upward splash, particularly when the pails are half-full or less. Not the case today.

When we finish gathering, we measure some six hundred gallons of sap in the storage tanks, about one quart of sap per tap. We expect the boil-off will net us about fifteen gallons of pure maple syrup.

Chapter Five

BOILING OFF

The first firing of Jackson Mountain Maple Farm's new Leader Special comes the same day as the sap gathering. Brud decides to boil off the sap while the volunteers and sightseers are still here. Similar to a preflight check of an airplane, he inspects the storage tanks, confirms that all evaporator plugs and fittings are in place, charges the firebox with birch bark and kindling, and then fills it loosely with birch edges.

We buy wood to fire the evaporator. We buy it at local sawmills, truck it up Jackson Mountain, and stack it outside the saphouse. We buy it and truck it while Hellgren and his woodchoppers cut beech and ash and now and again a maple tree all around us and truck the timber off down Jackson Mountain to a sawmill or paper mill some place. We buy wood because it's our best deal. We hardly have time to sugar, certainly no time to spend in the woods with a chain saw and fashion the thirty cords of firewood it will take to boil off seven hundred gallons of maple syrup. So we buy and burn waste edges from a sawmill in New Vineyard—or West Farmington.

Before Brud ignites his charge, he opens a valve and lets sap flow into the evaporator until the bottom of the pans are covered with about an inch of the sugary liquid. He then sets a float valve that will regulate the depth of sap at about one inch, or a bit less, while it's boiling. Voter tells us that shallow sap is the goal. Shallow sap produces lighter and tastier syrup, and produces it quicker. Brud's one inch is the popular depth, Voter tells him, but one inch will require him to be attentive to the boiling.

The saphouse is full of spectators. In addition to the volunteer gatherers and sightseers taking pictures at this historic event, Hellgren is here with Fontaine and Bergeron, his logging crew. Fontaine, a veteran Quebec sugarmaker, describes to some of the spectators what is going on. Warren Voter, the Leader sales agent, is here too; he's here to look over the setup and guide the new rig's operation. He explains how to judge when the syrup is nearing the draw-off point, what the foam will look like, how the liquid will sheet off the edge of a scoop—observations he's accumulated from a lifetime of sugaring.

Warren Voter is the only commercial maple producer I know. I have been to his saphouse, located in a well-kept maple grove on Voter Hill in West Farmington, once. Voter farms near the top of a hill named for his ancestors, up a road so long and steep that the first successful attempt by an automobile to get to the top under its own power—a Hudson— required, as the story goes, the use of reverse gear, and was reported in *The Franklin Journal*, the local newspaper. Voter produces dairy products and maple syrup up there—as did his father, Arthur, before him—in a 1,200-taphole maple grove that yields some four hundred gallons of maple syrup in a decent year. But it was Voter's other maple doings that brought him notability.

Voter, unexplainably perhaps, and possibly not recognized at the time, was a forward maple thinker. He participated on the leading edge of Maine's attempt to organize and grow the industry. A member of the Franklin County Maple Syrup Producers in 1947, before the statewide association was formed, Warren—and Arthur—joined the Maine Maple Producers Association as charter members in 1948. He subsequently served as president and director of the fledgling association multiple years, alongside Ken Cooper and Richard Eaton, shaping the organization into the maple syrup advocate it would become. He was the first in Maine to promote the use of plastic tubing for sap collection, albeit unsuccessfully at first. And as a member of the Franklin County Board of

Commissioners, the innovative Voter promotes Franklin County maple syrup to everyone he encounters as he travels throughout the county.

Voter produces an outsized amount of syrup from his 1,200-taphole orchard, and is able to move it all—and more—himself. The Forster Manufacturing Company, manufacturer of thirty-some woodenware items at their factories in Strong and Wilton—toothpicks, clothespins, coffee stirrers, and the like—purchases custom-packaged maple syrup for customer gifts. Voter has the account.

Voter also markets Leader Evaporator Company equipment and supplies to maple producers throughout the state. And he represents several can manufacturers also, including the distribution of the coveted Maine blue, white, and red–labeled container. Voter has purchased sap from Brud the past few years and likely other sap producers as well, sap that the progressive Voter paid for with shares of syrup. Jackson Mountain Maple Farm has purchased equipment from Voter—containers, too—and seeks advice and consent from him as well. It is consent we're looking for when we light up our new firebox for the first time.

Voter confirms that the level of sap in the pans is about right, and that we have sufficient sap in the storage tanks to likely reach a temperature of 219°F at the draw before we run out of sap. He nods to Brud, and Brud ignites the kindling with a wooden match and a piece of birch bark. After about twenty minutes with the front draft open, the evaporator is roaring, sap is bubbling, and the saphouse is filling with steam rising off the pans and up through the rafters, reaching for the roof vents above.

The Leader Special maple syrup evaporator is no easy rig for first-timers to operate. Though it is proven evaporator technology and is used in saphouses throughout the maple world, not one of us on Jackson Mountain save Voter has operated one or, as in my case, even seen one until we put the pieces of this one in the back of a truck in Burlington a month ago. We own the latest model. It comprises three pans in a series: a preheater or small warming pan, a flue pan that sits over the rear eight feet of the arch, and a flat pan that sits over the firebox at the front. The flat pan, or syrup pan as it's usually called, takes up the first six feet of the fourteen-foot arch, the flue pan the remaining eight. Draft created by a high stack at the rear sweeps the fire through the flues and heats the entire boiling rig uniformly.

Brud is anxious, as he should be. He watches and walks and watches and walks, continually checks the depth of sap and inspects the boiling temperature at the draw, the hottest point in the process. A dial thermometer with its probe inserted into the syrup pan at the draw, set at 0°F just as fresh sap had started to boil, indicates the boiling temperature. Target temperature is 7°F.

As the sap heats, Voter coaxes Brud to "throw in a few more edges." He says not to let the fire ebb, but to keep it uniformly hot by frequent and quick stoking. After about an hour of boiling, the temperature hovers a bit above 6°F at the draw. "Toss a little chicken-feed in under the draw," Voter orders. "See what that does." The quick heat moves the pointer just enough to reach the needed seven degrees. Brud dials the draw-off valve to open, and a gallon of maple syrup, perhaps two, drops into a tin milking-parlor pail before the temperature at the draw drops enough to close the valve. It's our first bit of pure syrup, and it comes about two hundred years after the first pure maple syrup produced in the District of Maine by Stephen Titcomb, who boiled it off in a kettle hanging over an open fire in what is now Farmington. But Titcomb's old cast iron kettle is long ago retired. Today's syrup is boiled off in a modern arrangement of tin pans.

Syrup is made continuously in the Leader Special. No batches. When the rig is running smoothly, a constant supply of cold sap flows into the upstream pan, the warming pan, and a constant volume of finished maple syrup—say one-fortieth of the incoming volume of cold sap—comes off at the draw point. It's a balancing act, a tightrope stretched between the sap storage tank and the wood pile. When one runs out the other must be stopped.

We boil another two hours. I wonder, while Brud paces back and forth and back and forth, are we running short of sap? Or do we need more wood? Is the rig in equilibrium? Get it wrong and, as they say, "all hell will break loose." I'm tense about it. Sap is boiled fast in the Leader Special, in our case some two hundred gallons per hour, three or so gallons per minute. It will take time to slow this rig down.

But Brud charges forward, confident now, like a jockey on the clubhouse turn. The goal is to boil off all the sap we've collected. The rig is balanced. Just enough of a continuous flow of fresh sap flows into the warming pan to replace the boiled-off steam and the drawn-off syrup. Occasionally, he changes a float setting, bringing in slightly more—or less—sap according to how deep the boiling liquid measures at the draw, or how much is flowing out of the warming pan. But the adjustments are few—and slight. Mostly, he routinely adds a charge of edges to the fire and lets the eight-foot flue pan do the work of converting sap to syrup.

Flue pans were first used by sugarmakers in the late 1800s, and likely came to Maine a bit later. Mrs. Nellie Titcomb Williams, who with her husband, Charles, operated Maple Hill Fruit Farm in Farmington, first made syrup on a complete set of continuous-flow evaporator pans soon after the turn of the twentieth century. She termed the flue-pan evaporator a "wonderful invention" that produced "delicious" maple syrup. Mrs. Williams, of course, remembered when producers boiled sap in a two-barrel—sixty-three gallons or one hogshead—potash kettle set in a brick arch. The potash kettle required repeated additions of sap to prevent scorching, thus producing a hefty flavored syrup. She acknowledged that quick boiling on a modern multipan evaporator produced "much better" tasting maple syrup, and lighter in color.

To make a flue pan, manufacturers bent the bottom sheet of metal—tin was commonly used to manufacture pans in the late 1800s—into longitudinal flues six or so inches deep and an inch or so wide for the sap to flow through, thus increasing the area of hot metal surface exposed to sap some fivefold, and the evaporation rate a similar amount. A Quebec inventor, David Ingalls of East Durham, shaped the first flue pan in 1889 by bending a sheet of tin over a length of railroad track to form the flues. In 1893, the G. H. Grimm Manufacturing Company of Hudson, Ohio, a manufacturer of sugaring equipment, began marketing—for $100 Canadian—the Champion evaporator, an evaporator incorporating the first commercially produced flue pan, a milestone event in the evolution of sugaring technology. The flue pan enabled producers to increase their resource to as many as four thousand tapholes, and finish boiling a day's run before midnight. Boiling off maple syrup became a part-time job.

Following the first boil-off, we filter the hot syrup and package it in gallon cans, thirteen of them, and grade it medium amber. The C. F. Hodgkins General Store in the village has told us they'll set it on the counter when they open Monday and price it for sale at $5.95 per gallon. We are in the syrup business.

Our first season, however, is not everything we have dreamed. First, we produce a total of only 220 gallons of maple syrup, a meager amount considering that we set our sights on 700. Though the first run was timely and generous, two weeks pass before we make another drop. In addition, snow and cold air hang over Temple during all of mid-March, prime time for sugaring in the hills. And then another snowy and cold five days at the end of March sets us back even more. In spite of the bad weather, however, a rush of sap in April, enough to make 140 gallons of syrup, salvages our season—and directs our attention to other problems.

We are continually frustrated by high production costs. We fail to accurately predict the cost of sap collection; that is, the logging crew. And our plan to gather sap and produce syrup only on weekends turns out to be impossible. The fifteen-quart buckets, too small to hold even two days' sap run, force us to put the logging crew to work on weekdays, a significant upswing in our expected operating expense. The extra crew time wrecks our cash balance—meaning we don't have any—and thwarts our aggressive approach to rein in expenses. Paying more to collect the sap than its value, we learn, is actually counterproductive. More sap, more cost. And syrup prices do not support the cost of a hired gathering system. Labor costs are devastating us.

The Leader Special, however, turns out to be as advertised: six gallons of syrup per hour. Bur the birch edges prove troublesome. They produce a high temperature under the syrup pan and call for caution. The tin cannot be safely overheated. Tin requires ample sap in the pan all the time. It needs ample sap to insulate the bottom from extreme temperature lest the syrup overheat. Unfortunately, it happens to us. The edges burn hot, the sap goes to syrup and more, and we fail to keep it moving. The syrup overheats and thickens. A pungent odor fills the saphouse. The pan burns. It's damaged, wrinkled, puckered. We don't know whether it's serviceable, whether the crumpled bottom will allow syrup to flow to the draw—or not.

Brud calls Voter. Voter climbs the mile-long hill the next day to take a look and counsel us, as he had promised when we bought the rig. I suspect he knew then we'd surely burn a pan. He assesses the damage and says the burned pan will "prob'ly work okay" but that we "need to have a spare on hand." He suggests he have Leader make us a spare. Brud agrees.

Later in the season another hot fire shoots up the stack—likely too much draft—and sets the roof ablaze where the stack pokes through. I climb a ladder up into the rafters—twice—with a gallon of sap in a pail and smother the fire with well-aimed tosses of 2° Brix into the rafters. Crisis over, but the heat produced by the birch edges remains troublesome. The edges produce fire so hot we daren't leave it. A fire so hot that we're required to work two extra hours each night and shovel untold amounts of snow into the firebox to cool the coals, lest the sap left in the pan turn to charcoal during the night. So far, our first season is marked by hot fires, late nights, and meager production. And there's more.

Hiking out after a long day and night of making syrup, carrying our paraphernalia in our arms, and packing syrup on our backs doesn't appeal to us after midnight. So every now and then we sleep—similar to the restless nap in the Burlington Laundromat—on the saphouse floor or on the counter that runs the length of one wall, a somewhat crude throwback to the nineteenth century when sugarmakers camped in the deep woods for weeks, boiled off their annual run of maple sap, and returned home carrying their crop of sugar and syrup on their backs. We carry our syrup out of the woods, too, some on our backs and the remainder in a box sitting on Hellgren's bulldozer. But we get the job done, and I'm fundamentally satisfied with the outcome. But getting there is hard work.

Our cash account is troublesome as well. The 220 gallons of pure Maine maple syrup, barely enough to satisfy our egos, is not even close to the premise we based this endeavor on, seven hundred gallons of syrup and a handsome cash profit. Nor is it even enough to make the small payment I'd promised the bank. As it turns out, we sell the syrup for $6 per gallon and $2 per quart, pay the operating bills, and the money is gone. On my way to the bank to plead guilty of misrepresentation and dicker for more money, I meet James Flint, bank president, crossing the street on his way to lunch. "How was the sugar season?" he asks.

I blurt it out. "I came to pay you the five hundred, Mr. Flint, but I don't have it. Bad year. I need to borrow another five hundred instead."

Flint smiles a bit like he might have known what would happen and offers his apologies. "See Hawkins," he tells me. "He'll fix you up with what you need." Munroe Hawkins, bank vice president and functional equal of Flint, treats me as Flint said he would. I breathe a sigh of relief and go away.

I didn't know then whether the $500 would be enough or not. I did know, however, that for us to make any money at sugaring, we need to be better organized, have a plan, create a budget, be more efficient, and control our costs. On the other hand, Brud posts a short blurb in *News from the Bush*, a seasonal sugaring publication the Maine Department of Agriculture distributes to maple syrup producers, asking whether any producer has surplus syrup for sale. He wants to buy syrup. But neither Brud's plan nor mine will produce profit. Our passion for big sugaring will prevent it.

Chapter Six

FREEZING NIGHTS AND FREEZING DAYS

IT'S 1965, A NEW YEAR. WE'RE BROKE. IN JANUARY, BRUD AND I, MEM-bers now of the Maine Maple Producers Association, drive to Lewiston to the MMPA's annual meeting at the armory, part of the Lewiston Agricultural Trade Show. It's the first time for the MMPA at the Lewiston show, and the first anywhere for Brud and me. I go to learn what happens at these events. Brud, though we have no money, is there to dicker for surplus maple syrup.

Thirty or so people show up, mostly a collection of veteran producers from western and central Maine. The topical agenda includes numerous items; for example, last year's production results, prospects for the coming spring, potential outlets for syrup, tapping dates, a price discussion, budget business, and the election of new officers. A maple production clinic for Maine sugarmakers is planned for the afternoon. Ralph Hilton, who makes pure Maine maple syrup in an Anson saphouse built in 1883, is president, elected a year ago in the New Sharon Grange Hall. Ted Harding, an Athens sugarmaker considered by his peers to be Maine's largest producer of syrup and syrup products—Harding is Maine's paramount maple candy maker—is vice president. William "Bucky" Buckland, maple specialist at the Department of Agriculture and author pro tempore of *News from the Bush*, is secretary. Hilton runs the meeting.

Alex Dickson, extension forester at Cornell University, is keynote speaker. His subject, "Modernizing the Maple Business," is an attempt to apply automation to collecting sap. Such subjects as pressure pumps, piping sap, creative uses of gravity, and applied vacuum appear on his

39

agenda, items that I don't yet need to know more about. Next is a panel discussion on central processing, which seems to me to be adding even more cost to sap collection. The day's most interesting topic, however, is when producers are polled anonymously for anticipated 1965 prices. Average per gallon price for Fancy or grade A syrup in 1965, according to the poll, figures to be $7.

Other business follows. Warren Voter, dealer in maple supplies, reports that eighty-five thousand paraformaldehyde pellets have been ordered for the 1965 season. At least two producers in the Four Hundred Club—those who produce more than four hundred gallons of maple syrup in a year—announce bulk syrup for sale. Last is an announcement of the winners of the annual maple syrup contest. When the meeting breaks up, Brud bandies with some Four Hundred Club members over the price of bulk surplus syrup, while I inquire of Hilton how to submit a sample of syrup for the contest. At the end, we leave energized for the coming spring. "It's a whole new season." Brud exclaims. "Maybe we can win a few."

The Old Farmer's Almanac is persistent that the first sap run will come on March 10. The temperature turns cold near the end of February, however, and stays cold, dampening our spirits some, and we put off the start of tapping until March 6. When March 6 comes, a Saturday, Hellgren and his dozer distribute buckets through the woods in just a half-day. We—Brud, Bill, I, and whomever Brud can cajole to come here from the frat house—drill holes, insert pellets, drive spouts, hang buckets, and put on covers. We work two weekends and finish the job March 14. At the end of the second weekend, three thousand buckets hang on Hellgren's trees waiting for sap. Unfortunately and contrary to the information in *The Old Farmer's Almanac*, the temperature continues its February routine: freezing nights and freezing days.

We wait, but sap doesn't show. Mid-March, no sap. Brud drives to Temple from Orono. "Maybe I can make it run," he boasts with a grin. But the sap doesn't run, won't run. Brud returns to Orono and taps a sugar maple on the lawn of Phi Eta Kappa. I drive to my place in Augusta to work—and worry. We have identified perhaps four hundred gallons in sales, a huge increase over the first year that we attribute to being licensed producers—and better known. Orders for syrup arrive in Temple almost daily. Brud, impatient, sees a bit of sap in the bucket hanging at Phi Eta Kappa and he's soon back in Temple. But it goes on. We wait, and I worry.

Lower costs are not accidental, I mull, and I try to persuade Brud in advance of the first run to change our gathering strategy, hold off the dozer and the crew a bit until the buckets are full, perhaps some even overfull. We have virtually no cash, I tell him, nothing to pay for the dozer and a crew, unless they can come up with a thousand gallons or more of sap. "Wait for 'em to fill up," I say. He agrees. We'll let the sap run and focus on the weekends.

First sap run in Temple comes the last week in March, a continuous run of sap that stretches our ability to stay with it. And the run continues intermittently well into April. Last sap arrives on April 20, less than four weeks since the first run. Beth—my bride-to-be—and I hike up to the saphouse on a warm Sunday afternoon and boil off the sap in the tank to ten gallons of syrup, ending the season. Final 1965 syrup production is just a bit less than three hundred gallons, a goodly sum but still far short of seven hundred and one hundred less than the orders we expect to get. Brud advertises again in *News from the Bush* and makes a few phone calls to members of the Four Hundred Club. His effort comes up with 150 gallons. "It's been a good season in Maine," he says. "Price is down."

We struggle to sell the syrup. Brud's wholesale market doesn't emerge to the extent we hope for. Seems all Maine producers enjoy abundant production. No surplus buyers. We are certain to have syrup on our hands this summer. I call Voter, thinking he might take some syrup for his Forster account, syrup he packs in Forster Manufacturing's cans. Though Voter has likely produced a bumper crop as well, I know he sometimes solicits syrup from surrounding producers for the toothpick account. "We have some syrup on hand," I tell him, "suppose we could fill some of the Forster cans for you?"

Voter balks. Producers of his generation, I'm learning—Titcomb, Small, Fronk, and Voter, too—are fussy about the syrup they sell. They produce the best and that's what they want to sell. Voter has a reputation to protect. "Is it good syrup?" he asks.

"Medium grade," I tell him. "We pack it in the Maine can. I'll bring you over a quart to taste."

"Never mind that," he says. "I'll let you have a case of empties. I'll taste one of those."

I take Warren one hundred quarts, twenty-five gallons of the best-tasting syrup we've made yet. He's happy. So am I.

Later, Brud somehow sells the remaining syrup and I pay the bills. Nothing is left over, no syrup, no cash. The bank has to wait again. The cost of gathering sap, I figure, though somewhat improved by the decision to work the logging crew less, continues to drag us down. I make a final accounting and determine that our three-hundred-gallon production costs us $6.96 per gallon to make and package, something less than in 1964. We sell gallons now for $6.95.

When the season ends I'm tired. I need a break from all this. I see a notice in the April issue of *News from the Bush* hyping the coming of the 7th Annual Maine Maple Festival and Sugaring-Off Party in Strong. The festival, sponsored jointly by the Strong Lions Club, the Maine Maple Producers Association, and the Department of Agriculture, will, says the *News*, be held in Strong, Maine, on Saturday, April 18, and feature bands, dog sled rides, and sugar on snow. Also appearing at the festival, the *News* tempts its readers, will be the 1963 Maine and New England Maple Queen, Paula Wing of Portland. The *News* also reports that a new queen will be crowned at this much-heralded event. It's all held at the Forster—the toothpick tycoon—Memorial Hall on Saturday, April 18. Though not mentioned, the Maple Festival also offers refuge from the incessant gnawing of slimy galvanized buckets sitting outside my saphouse on Jackson Mountain. I go to the festival.

I don't go to espy the queen contestants or to show off my maple syrup to the judges there or to hobnob with big-boy producers Orlando Small, Ted Harding, and the rest of the Four Hundred Club. I go because my only alternative is washing sap buckets with Brud and the buddies he brings from Orono to "do some old-fashioned sugaring." I can't face the buckets.

The Franklin Journal reports that hundreds of people will crowd the streets and halls of Strong for the festival. An early-bird baked bean dinner at the Aurora Grange kicks off the festivities at noon. Next is a long parade. The parade route stretches along Main Street from the Foster Memorial Building to the Strong School, maybe a mile. Onlookers stand two-deep along the curb eyeing color guards, drum and bugle corps, troops of boy scouts and girl scouts, George Worthley and his Timberline Huskies fresh from having trotted in the recent Inaugural Parade in Washington, D.C., and the eight candidates for 1965 Maine Maple Queen. The newest in farming and lumbering equipment, chain saws and motorboats, and the new 1965 model automobiles are also on display—at the schoolhouse.

Throughout the afternoon, Worthley and his sled dogs offer free rides to giggling children, Lew Badershall ekes out Richard Pinkham in a saw-off for the fastest chain saw in the county, and the Bucks and Does from Richmond put on a square dance demonstration for the cheering sugarmakers. At the same time, Barbara Allen, WCSH-TV Channel 6 television emcee of the weekly *Youth Cavalcade*, hosts teenage auditions for the show, while Pete Daigle of Sinclair, whose own saphouse queen, Miss Bernadette Sinclair, is a contestant in the state contest, stages a bit of entertainment himself: a short movie of maple syruping in Sinclair. And all the while Maple House, a local syrup outlet, serves maple syrup, maple syrup candy, maple syrup on ice cream, and maple syrup on snow.

An Aunt Jemima pancake banquet—pure Maine maple syrup and Maine sausages—and the coronation ball top off the day. More than three hundred people jam into the Randall Thomas Gymnasium for the banquet. Following the pancakes, WLAM Lewiston-Auburn radio personality Fred Gage introduces Merritt Caldwell from the Department of Agriculture who announces results of the 1965 Maine maple syrup contest. Top honor for best maple syrup out of thirty entrants, Caldwell announces, goes to Raymond Titcomb of Farmington; second to Nelson Fronk of Farmington; third to Foster and Williams of Skowhegan; and fourth, to W. H. and L. E. Cook of Phillips.

Gage introduces 1963 Maine and New England Maple Queen Paula Wing, 1964 New England Maple Queen Bonnie Lee Murray of Auburn, and announces that the judges have selected Miss Marilyn Yeaton, a senior at Farmington High School and a National 4-H award winner,

1965 Maine Maple Queen. MMPA President Ralph Hilton of Anson, assisted by Paula Wing, positions the tiara on the new queen's head. The Earl Myers orchestra of Wilton strikes up the first bars of the coronation ball, and folks close out the evening and the 1965 maple season on the dance floor while I drive back to Temple. I will learn tomorrow whether Brud has the buckets washed.

The first Annual Maine Maple Festival and Sugaring-Off Party, also in Strong, was held in 1959 during a time when Maine producers sought to bring attention to their growing maple industry, increase their sales, and broaden their presence as a New England producer. Maple production in Maine had shown little growth in the years leading up to 1959, hovering at about eight or nine thousand gallons annually, down considerably since 1950 when thirty thousand gallons were reported produced in Maine.

Producers sought more visibility in 1959. The industry was poised to grow and convinced festival sponsors Maine Maple Producers Association, Strong Lions Club, and the Maine Department of Agriculture to take a step upward. Technology change had also begun to come to the industry. Warren Voter was introducing plastic tubing; Ray Titcomb and others were tapping more and trying alternate fuels, early signs of a turnaround. Unfortunately, growth in syrup production did not respond. The annual festival, perhaps the first gala since MMPA adopted bylaws defining their mission as promoting Maine Maple Syrup, lasted eight years. The final show played in 1967. The sponsors had run out of energy.

It is about this time, April 1965, the end of the second punishing year on Jackson Mountain, that Brud proposes buying a horse. "Pick up some old nag for a song," he says. He tells me we could get a wagon too, ride up to the saphouse and carry the syrup back in the wagon. "Maybe a race horse," he adds. "We could run him at the county fairs in the fall. What's a farm without a horse, anyway?" He complains again and again of the aches and pains he acquires from his two-mile hike up the mountain. He says we should pave the old settler road the two miles from Dooley's to the saphouse.

Brud's rant is my first clue that he is getting tired of Jackson Mountain. That the work is getting to him. Most of our effort, most of our energy, is taken up by the to and fro of the enterprise—tap and collect, boil and package, transport and sell. And except for a sputtering gas lantern that threatens to blow the saphouse to smithereens, our work is in the cold and the dark. Working conditions are sucking the life out of us. But I have no desire to quit. I may go broke or get injured, but quitting is not an alternative.

We do not acquire a horse—or pave the road. Nor do aches and pains drive our decision making. Yes, we're tired—and broke as well. But it is the expense that's defeating us. Unable to pay down our debt—in fact, we increase it—or timely pay our operating costs, we decide to give up our stake on Jackson Mountain and seek a new opportunity.

But first we pay our debts. We owe the bank the annual payment, perhaps two. In September when the apples ripen the payment is still staring us in the face. Temple was an apple-growing town in the nineteenth century, and apples are still plentiful in September on the abandoned farm sites. We—Brud and Bill—resurrect Howard Mitchell's old cider mill next to Temple Stream on the intervale road, gather apples from the outback farms, and chop and squeeze them into apple cider. The cider, produced over a period of perhaps two months and packaged for sale in fifty-gallon wooden barrels for local cellars, pays our operating bills and covers a payment at the bank. Apple cider saves Jackson Mountain from bankruptcy—or perhaps worse. "What's a farm without a cider mill?" I ask. Brud smiles. Solvency puts us back into a hopeful mood.

The two years on Jackson Mountain produced mostly memories. We made a modest amount of maple syrup and received more for it—publicity, friendships, and a meager amount of cash—than perhaps we deserved. And we discovered the reasons why we shouldn't have gone there. It was a difficult, almost impossible, location; we had no money;

not one of us had time to invest in the enterprise; sugaring on Jackson Mountain required more work than we could collectively do. Yes, we were tired much of the time, but it was the unexpectedly high expenses that spelled the end. Apple cider rescued us.

We also learned in those two brief years that the biggest challenge in efficient sugarmaking is found not inside the saphouse but outside in the woods. The inside cost to boil off a gallon of maple syrup is pretty much a fixed number and predictable with some accuracy. The outside cost to produce the sap varies with weather and time and is, of course, unpredictable. Gathering sap timely and efficiently without losing any to weather or spillage is where the great challenge lies. We learned that on Jackson Mountain. Now we need to learn what to do about it.

We're still in the sugaring business, though. We'll figure it out.

DAY MOUNTAIN ROAD

LATE SUMMER 1965. BRUD WRITES ME FROM ORONO. HE HAS A PLAN. "We're moving Jackson Mountain Maple Farm," he writes. "Moving everything, building, equipment, tools, supplies, and even the name of the place. We're moving four miles down Day Mountain Road onto an acre of land we'll buy from Hellgren."

Day Mountain Road, I know, has all the geographical advantages we lacked on Jackson Mountain. Brud cites many of them in his missive. We will benefit from easy access to the village—three miles of paved road—and onsite electricity. A water supply, a small brook that runs full in the spring but trickles near empty in the summer and fall, crosses the land less than fifteen yards from the front door of the proposed saphouse. "We'll tap roadside trees," Brud writes. "Make a deal with the owners in exchange for syrup, collect the sap ourselves with the Chevy truck."

The bottom line is that the site will require less labor than Jackson Mountain did and less gathering costs than we paid Hellgren's crew. And traffic will pass by our place, perhaps bringing us onsite sales. "We couldn't be better off," Brud writes, "and should we choose to, we can go back to the mountain later—with an expansion plan."

But for now we go back to the beginning and start over. We have nothing to show for our efforts on the mountain but a debt at the bank, all because we couldn't predict the cost of sap gathering up there. But Hellgren has his sugar maples back, and his logging crew as well. And though I feel a bit sad that he will lose the income, I expect he made a tad of profit on the sale of the acre.

Sap gathering has been an aggravation for maple producers since the discovery that maple sap contained sugar. Sap gathered tree to tree from a disorganized multitude of sugar maples must somehow be brought together at a boiling place. It's the bringing together, the conveying, that causes economic—time and money—stress. Whether boiled on a kitchen stove, or atop an outdoor fireplace, or in a commercial evaporator, transporting sap gathered tree to tree to a fire somehow prevents most producers from efficient and profitable management of the routine. Backyard producers, those who limit their sugaring to producing syrup for their own needs, aren't as likely to be overly aggravated collecting sap from trees on the back lawn. But commercial producers, whether using oxen or a pickup truck, or whether collecting in the woods or along a paved highway, have seldom had adequate time or sufficient money to conduct a tight and efficient gathering operation. Nor have they been tempted to expand their sugarbushes to any great degree.

Helen Nearing had the same problem over in Vermont in the 1940s and wrote about it in *The Maple Sugar Book*. "With a moderate length of haul," she wrote, "it will take from two to five times as long to take the gathering tank to the saphouse and back again as it did to fill the tank." Her frustrations with trying to overcome this costly and aggravating necessity of collecting sap tree to tree led her to try gravity. But she couldn't make it work. In her case, a network of three-quarter-inch galvanized piping laid on the ground and fed through standpipes eventually fell victim to excessive maintenance and Vermont freeze-ups.

Gravity, of course, was the right answer for her, as well as others. But producers had tinkered with gravity for years without any substantial success. Since the mid-1800s such appurtenances as wooden troughs and tin piping and gutter spouts and iron water pipes had been constructed or erected or installed between sugar grove and saphouse in futile attempts to transport sap out of the tree directly to a distant boiling pan. As far back as 1793, according to Nearing, handmade wooden piping was used in a tree-to-tree system, but it was soon abandoned because it cracked or warped or otherwise failed. Maine producer Ted Greene in Sebago tells of his ancestors using metal troughs to run sap from tree to tree to the storage tank in the 1800s. Metal piping had been attempted by others, as well, but none had demonstrated sufficient reliability or capacity to gain any widespread approval—or longevity. Most were doomed at the outset.

Perhaps the most successful application of gravity—and the most work—was one of the many attempts by the Nearings. In 1935, as it's told in *The Maple Sugar Book*, they opted against the tree-to-tree system and fashioned an aerial network of three-quarter-inch tin piping arranged on a sloping site that also included collection tanks at the upper end that gatherers brought sap to, then running it through aerial pipelines to the saphouse. They experimented five years with this system, making various adjustments and adding accoutrements—running sap through aerial tin troughs on a uniform gradient, removing ice and snow, replacing troughs with pipelines and vice versa, plugging insistent leaks, and experimenting with the height of the lines—until they finally settled on iron pipeline laid on the ground surface.

They struggled with this arrangement for ten more years, adding pieces of radiator hose to absorb expansion and allow contraction, supporting lines where necessary with wire and edgings. At the end of ten years the maintenance of the system had become overbearing, and they gave in to it. In 1952, the Nearings abandoned sugaring and moved to the Maine coast, where they grew vegetables and harvested wild blueberries. Pipeline snags, snow, ice, and winter rains had taken away the joys of sugaring, their gravity piping system consigned to history.

In 1966, effective and widespread use of gravity for sap gathering had not reached Maine, or anyplace else, in any substantive way. Gathering systems then, as they had for almost two hundred years, required excessive energy, time, and money. Producers gathered daily to prevent the sap from spoiling or freezing in the buckets—splitting seams as well—and trapping mice and red squirrels under the ice. The benefits of daily gathering for those who practiced it, however, also included a higher-grade maple syrup. The sap was fresher and cleaner and produced a lighter color, and the syrup tasted better.

At the Day Mountain Road boiling site, lacking other alternatives, we plan a roadside gathering system, a tank on the back of a truck. Temple bears a lengthy network of country and backcountry roads. The labyrinth reaches the limits of the town and, in places, loops and reverses and goes on for perhaps twenty miles through Temple's hills. Intervale Road, Day Mountain Road, Iisalo Road, Orchard Hill Road, and Varnum Pond Road are all lined with mature and leafy maples replete with sugar, all on private property. On front lawns of occupied residences, side yards of abandoned hill-farms, edges of cow pastures and hay fields, and in small roadside groves, sugar maples with large crowns, high sugar contents, and easy access, save an occasional non-navigable snowbank, exist. We estimate 1,500 tapholes are available.

Throughout the summer, Brud negotiates permission from the land-owners, our new partners, to tap the designated trees. Those who accept his offer agree to receive a fair share of the syrup. He also comes to an agreement with his father, owner of the Hodgkins General Store in the village, on the use of the old red Chevy delivery truck to gather and convey the sap, it no longer needed to deliver sundries to distant store customers. "He won't need it to deliver groceries," Brud tells us, "so it's ours now," and he paints "Jackson Mountain Maple Farm" on both doors.

We lift a nine-barrel gathering tank up onto the Chevy's back. Brud tells Bill and me that the Chevy is not registered, and we must limit its use to the farm, which now consists of a one-acre plot of land on Day Mountain Road and about twenty miles of public right-of-way fifty feet wide. Our gathering costs—gasoline for the truck and our own volunteer time—are expected to plummet from our two-year experience on Jackson Mountain, resulting in a tidy profit—for the first time.

A roadside sugarbush is not groundbreaking technology. They've been around a long time, probably since the creation of a road system and the coming of the pickup truck—or the trailer hitch. Accessibility and suitable transportation make roadside trees desirable. As does the higher sugar contents that come with well-crowned, leafy sugar maples that grow in open spaces. The amount of sugar and starch in a sugar maple tree is directly proportional to the number and the size of the leaves. The leaves all photosynthesize—produce starch—in October and November. The starch turns to sugar during the dead of winter.

The makeup of roadside sugarbushes in Maine—and elsewhere— varies considerably. In 1944 I tapped three trees along Cowturd Lane in Temple, carried the sap into the house in a pail, and Ma boiled it off to syrup on the kitchen stove. In 1964 Bob Smith, owner of Smith Maple Products in Skowhegan, put in 1,800 roadside taps—he paid twenty-five cents per taphole—in Skowhegan, Norridgewock, Fairfield, Cornville, and Madison, gathered the sap into a tank on a U-Haul trailer, and boiled it off in a saphouse on Silver Street in downtown Skowhegan. Ed Jillson in Sabattus has tapped roadside trees in Androscoggin, Kennebec, and Sagadahoc counties for years. Mike Smith in Winthrop empties buckets after work from his neighbors' lawns.

Sugarmakers who choose to tap the roadside must also cope with the risks. Landowners will want more syrup, or protest too many taps in a tree, or renounce the agreement. Sap somehow inexplicably becomes contaminated—beer bottles and dead mice are common—or the bucket has a bullet hole in it. Other roadside risks might include icy roads, high snowbanks, and speeding traffic. There's virtually no limit to what will happen once I leave our one-acre plot on Day Mountain Road to collect sap with the old red Chevy.

Brud writes to me again in February, this time news of his progress toward being ready for the first sap run in March, predicted again by *The Old Farmer's Almanac* to come on March 10. The new saphouse—a

collection of recycled boards and timbers gleaned from abandoned struc-
tures along Day Mountain Road—is up and closed in, and a platform
to hold up the storage tank is constructed beside it. The Leader Special,
he tells me, is safely tucked inside the new sapshack, where it rests on
wobbly legs after being dragged on its belly through snow drifts and
over stone walls down Day Mountain Road for some two days prior to
its arrival. "The drainpipe will need a spot of solder," Brud writes, "but
that's all." Later I drive to Temple to see the new setup and help Brud
nail down the final layer of roofing. I find the shack sitting in a hollow
about a mile up Day Mountain Road and some thirty feet from the small
brook Brud described as our source of washwater.

The saphouse, the assemblage of old boards and timbers nailed
together by Brud, is vintage. The tar paper finish is held in place by laths.
Boards expose cracks and gaps hither and yon that let air inside to boost
the fire. The stack protrudes from the roof maybe twelve feet. Windows
are nailed in place. A tilted flagpole decorates the front. There's not a
right angle or straight line anywhere. It's like Grandpa C. F. built this
place in 1890. It's beautiful.

The Leader Special, a veteran now of being jostled around like a dog
in the back of a pickup truck, sits inside on the geographic center of the
earthen floor, supported under its corners and legs by concrete blocks. A
screw jack is available for adjusting the arch to compensate for the ups
and downs of the freezing and thawing earth, common in this part of
Maine. Brud has built a counter along one wall. Electricity—no Coleman
gas lantern here—comes from an aged Cape Cod cottage sitting about
two hundred yards up Day Mountain Road, where Brud has stretched an
NM #12/2 electric wire, plugged one end into a receptacle in the cottage
cellar, and wired the other end to a receptacle on the saphouse counter.
For light, we stick the bare wires of a pigtail light into the saphouse
receptacle.

Outside, two thirty-barrel storage tanks sit on a platform tucked up
next to a bank that will allow the Chevy to pipe off its load by gravity.
Firewood—birch edgings from a New Vineyard sawmill again—sits outside the front door, handy to the firebox. The place looks to work well, I
think, and I'm expecting passersby to stop and talk and watch us boil off

the syrup, perhaps ask a question or two or maybe bring an extra bottle of ale inside and set it on the counter. I expect, too, that our sapshack will be a social stop on the way to and from the popular Big Don's roadhouse three miles up on Tater Mountain Road, the site of Temple's only ski resort. Perhaps even a Big Don's customer or two will stop in and pick up some syrup for Sunday pancakes. Our prospects look good here for a sociable 1966 maple syrup season.

Chapter Eight

THE SECRET IS HIDDEN IN THE LEAVES

WE START TAPPING THE FIRST WEEKEND IN MARCH. BRUD DRILLS THE tapholes, stumbling up and down snowplow banks, climbing over stone walls, at times working in snow up to his hips, at times walking in a rut-filled dirt road. I follow in his tracks, insert a spout, and hang a fifteen-quart bucket and a cover. The work is slow. It's a daylight job, and three days pass before it's done, 1,600 buckets. And we beat the sap run. Not until mid-March does the run come. It comes in prodigious amounts, though, and fills the buckets day after day after day.

The Chevy does its tree-to-tree job well, something akin to oxen. Uphill, side hill, through mud and snow it groans, a half-load of sap sloshing in the back. It doesn't cough or skip or weaken in any way. Maybe it will learn where to stop, and which side of the road has the buckets, I ruminate, while lifting a full pail of sap over my head and into the nine-barrel tank. The tank—280 gallons—is full before we're thirty minutes into the route. We take it to the storage tank and go back to the hills. Three more round trips and we have it done.

It's textbook sugaring. We boil late into the night, filter and package the syrup as we boil. The moon lights the landscape. Steam rises out of the roof and floats into the woods behind us, as does smoke from the stack. A passerby stops and comes in. "Cold nights and warm days is what causes this," I tell him.

"Should be 'nother good 'un tomorrow, too," he answers.

The season is looking good. The Chevy doesn't let us down, doesn't require maintenance, is ready every day when we show up to use it. It does whine occasionally for more gasoline, working as hard as it does pulling a full tank of sap up Day Mountain Road several times a day. But we don't take it off the farm for gas. We bring gas from West Farmington in a five-gallon can and pour it into the thirsty Chevy.

We learn that a nine-barrel gathering tank is small for the job. It takes us as many as four round trips into the hills to transfer the sap from the buckets to the storage tanks. Travel time from the trees to storage and back to the trees is lopsided, top heavy. We spend more time driving the truck than it takes to fill it with sap; typically it's late in the day before we can fire the arch. But we accept the deficiency and boil as late into the night as we need to. Three miles of paved road will get us home and into bed in less than fifteen minutes.

The five-foot-by-fourteen-foot Leader Special with the soldered drainpipe is also up to whatever we ask. We feed it birch edges, and it produces six gallons of pure maple syrup every hour. By the end of the season we have packed 350 gallons of Maine maple syrup in five different sizes of tin cans: gallon, half-gallon, quart, pint, and half-pint, our highest total yet. It's a pleasant surprise, and one that we are ready for.

We pack our 1966 syrup in lithographed all-state tin cans manufactured by the Stern Can Company in Peabody, Massachusetts, a first-rate company that makes high-quality F-style cans—some producers call them paint cans—at a reasonable price. In previous years we have packed syrup in the official blue, white, and red Maine-trademarked container, a popular can sanctioned by the Maine Department of Agriculture that many licensed Maine producers find beneficial to their sales. But we find them costly. Adequate inventory for unpredictable sales in each of five container sizes ties up too much money. So we switch to a commercially available lithographed can for half the price. We figure to save forty cents per gallon of syrup in packing costs. And we stick a name label on the can indicating that it's pure Maine maple syrup made in Temple by Jackson Mountain Maple Farm. Though we do miss the blue, white, and red symbol of Maine-made syrup, the stick-on label meets our promotional needs.

The Maine Department of Agriculture created the official blue, white, and red agricultural trademark in the 1930s during the Great Depression when the nation's economy was dormant and needed a boost. The department issued regulations and licenses authorizing agricultural growers and maple syrup producers to use the trademark on Maine grown and packaged farm produce. For a $1 licensing fee, farmers could use the trademark in the packaging and identification of Maine quality products: potatoes, blueberries, milk, baked beans, dry beans, maple syrup, and more. And the Boston and Maine Railroad Company painted boxcars carrying State of Maine agricultural products with the popular and patriotic colors as well. The iconic trademark proved trendy, provided visibility for Maine products, and attracted interest and additional customers.

In 1964, the first year of maple production at Jackson Mountain Maple Farm, the blue, white, and red logo had been available for perhaps twenty-five years, and was used by virtually all commercial maple producers. We, of course, paid the $1 fee, purchased custom lithographed containers with the Maine trademark labeling, and filled them with syrup meeting the Maine grading law. Customers loved the package—loved the syrup too. Tourists found the Maine trademark irresistible, essential to document their whereabouts and convince their neighbors back home that first-rate maple syrup was made elsewhere than Vermont. "Be sure you put the Jackson Mountain Maple Farm label on there," they'd caution us, "and made in Temple, Maine, too."

A few years later, however, the three-color, trademarked maple syrup can fell out of favor. Container manufacturers were reluctant to make it. Higher manufacturing costs required higher prices. Profits were squeezed to stay competitive, but suppliers couldn't realize a reasonable return without eventual increases. As a result, producers cut down on the number of Maine trademark cans they used. Though the trademark bags and boxes furnished for potatoes and blueberries and such other agricultural products were still popular, the maple syrup can lost favor with maple producers due to its high cost. Producers replaced it with a less costly version of tin can. Jackson Mountain Maple Farm eliminated the icon can from its inventory in 1966. By 1970, no maple syrup producer in Maine was using the blue, white, and red-trademarked can. The Maine-branded maple syrup containers had disappeared.

In 1966, we produce 350 gallons of maple syrup on Day Mountain Road. The sap comes from 1,600 roadside tapholes on a twenty-mile route through Temple's backcountry. Conversely, the year before in Hellgren's woodlot on Jackson Mountain, we produced three hundred gallons of maple syrup from three thousand tapholes. With but half as many tapholes, our roadside landscaping trees sitting in the sun and sporting huge, leafy, symmetrical crowns balanced on thirty-inch-diameter sugar maple boles produce considerably more syrup than Hellgren's forest with twice as many tapholes. The difference, scientists say, is hidden in the leaves.

Sugar maple trees with large, leafy crowns produce superior leaves, and more of them. More leaves mean more sap. Large leaves mean more sugar. It all happens in the fall and winter following the growing season. Photosynthesis, the formation of carbohydrates in chlorophyll-crammed tissues—leaves—takes place in the fall, and starch is stored in the trunks and roots of the dormant trees. In the dead of winter, when the forest is dark and cold and still, the starch is converted to sugar, the amount dependent on the amount of carbohydrates—the size and number of leaves. More leaves mean more sap. Large leaves mean more sugar.

Sap production per taphole varies as well. From day to day during the season according to the vagaries of ambient temperature and other variables, and year to year for much the same reasons, the characteristics of sugar maple sap change. Early in the season sap is sweet and plentiful, and lighter colored syrups are usually dominant. As the season wears on, tapholes are affected by several undesirable—so the sugarmakers think—daily events and produce less sugar: the sugar content, victim of dilution of the sugar in the xylem, drops; shorter cycles of freezing temperatures produce shorter sap runs; presence of live bacteria in the taphole constrains sap flow through the sidewall; and buds increase their demand for sugary sap. The presence of such variables is usually a precursor to less daily sugar. Daily temperatures, however, are the most critical variable in sap production and the most commonly understood as well. Freezing nights and thawing days are essential. Without freezing and thawing, there is no sap.

Sap flow is also affected by other factors, factors that perhaps have less influence and are less understood. The health and vigor of the tree is one example. Sick and dying trees, trees without vigor, don't possess the energy to grow large leaves, draw sap, or create ample sugar through photosynthesis. The size of a tree's crown, its exposure to sun and wind, and its taphole depth all have something to say about the volume of sap production. Still another vagary, and perhaps the least understood of all, is bacteria's affect on taphole performance. Bacteria in a healthy environment can seal the wall of a taphole in just a few days, and end a syrup season when the calendar—or *The Old Farmer's Almanac*—says it's only half done.

Chapter Nine

BACTERIA

"WE SHOULD BE PRODUCING MORE SYRUP FROM THESE TREES," I TELL Brud, following the 1966 season. "A quart of syrup per tap is not enough, and we don't make that much."

"We'll tap more trees," he answers.

"We don't need more trees," I counter. "We need less bacteria."

Bacteria are the bane of maple producers. Once the taphole is drilled, bacteria go to work immediately to heal the wound. If not prevented somehow from accessing the hole, bacteria will seal it within a month, and reduce the sap flow to half in about three weeks. Bacteria—*Pseudomonas geniculata*—are invisible, not just to Brud but to everyone. They are an affliction on sap production. Bacteria darken the syrup. Bacteria alter its color, and likely its flavor. Bacteria seal the tapholes' sidewalls and block sap flow. Bacteria emit an unseemly aura to the sugaring persona. Bacteria are the enemy. Heretofore, we've counterattacked in the war on bacteria with a pellet gun. On Temple's residential roads, however, we shun the pellet.

In 1964, when Jackson Mountain Maple Farm started sugaring, our to-buy equipment list, in addition to evaporator pans, galvanized buckets, storage tanks, filter tanks, and so on, included a pellet gun, a small, orange, plastic cylindrical container with a hollow gun barrel on one end and a plunger on the other. We used it to insert a pellet, a paraformaldehyde sanitizing tablet, into the taphole. The pellet, Voter told us, would be effective in keeping the taphole fresh, and sap would run freely throughout the sugaring season, thus preventing mischievous bacteria from sealing the taphole's sidewalls and blocking the sap flow. Though we used it in Hellgren's woodlot, we learn later that the pellet is a pesticide, and we now avoid its use on residential property.

R. N. Costilow, A researcher at Michigan State University, developed the paraformaldehyde sanitizing pellet in 1962 in response to the need for sugarmakers to keep the taphole free of microorganisms. His pellet contained 250 mg of paraformaldehyde, a polymer of formaldehyde. The US Food and Drug Administration approved its use in 1965. Jackson Mountain Maple Farm used it in 1964 and 1965. Since then, the pellet has become very popular—and controversial. Mariafranca Morselli, research professor at the University of Vermont, has branded the tablet risky and a threat to sugar maple trees. Maine producers generally deny any observed ill effects. Warren Voter, manufacturers' agent for maple supplies and containers, reports increasing sales of the pellets.

The alternatives to use of the pellet are few—and onerous. Prior to 1962 and researcher Cositlow's pellet, many producers took time in midseason to ream their tapholes, pull spouts, and freshen the inside walls with another pass of a bit or reaming tool. Reaming was laborious and tedious work for those who did it, but they knew the importance of keeping the sap flowing, and the risk of not doing so. As much as half a season could be lost.

Richard Eaton in East Corinth is an example. In a letter to Ken Cooper, secretary of the MMPA, in May 1946, Eaton groans about his failure to ream his holes. "It was really a good season," he wrote Cooper, "but I didn't manage it right." Eaton explains that he had failed to ream his four thousand tapholes and had lost a third of his crop to the pesky bacteria, while his neighbor, with only three thousand tapholes, reamed and made as much syrup as Eaton did.

But not every producer reamed. The Nearings, Mainers who had sugared in Vermont in the 1930s and 1940s, did not ream, nor, according to *The Maple Sugar Book*, did any of their neighbors. The Nearings did retap occasionally, however, and they tell of "making phenomenal amounts of syrup tapping a second time." Mainers seem to be reamers, though, and much like Eaton's neighbor, they freshen their tapholes midway through the season. We did not ream on Jackson Mountain. We used the pellet. We knew—Voter had told us—that without the pellet a sap run after midseason would produce only half, or less, of the earlier runs, and the loss would multiply as time went on. It was a financial matter with us. With no time to ream, and Hellgren's woodlot on death row waiting for an executioner to wield a double-bitted guillotine, or as in Hellgren's case a chain saw, we disregarded the long-term health of his trees, inserted a pellet, and captured all the sap. At the same time we provided the trees a temporary stay of execution until our lease expired. But when it came time to tap Temple's roadside trees, the choice of whether to sanitize or not sanitize had different implications.

Temple's roadside comprises about twenty miles of rural living, separated occasionally by a short stretch of forest. The roadside passes by sheep pastures and hayfields and apple orchards of the former hill-farmers, some still maintaining a slight resemblance to the distant past, and an assortment of single-family farmhouses built before the Great Depression. All the land is privately owned, much of it used, somehow, every day. The pellet, when we use it at all, is limited to the invisible trees, sugar maples that folks don't see when they look out their parlor windows or drive by Temple's hay fields. Three small sugar maple groves hidden in the woods out of sight produce sap for us as well, one on Orchard Hill Road, one on Varnum Pond Road, and one on Day Mountain Road. We dump the sap into a tin barrel and drain it downhill to the truck through a piece of plastic pipe. These three groves are candidates for the pellet, but the remaining sugar maples, the visible maples next to folks' lawns and side yards and alongside Temple's country roads, perhaps 80 percent of our roadside bush, are tapped without the pellet, or any other means of prohibiting the darned microbe from sealing the taphole. We try not to risk the health of Temple's landscape sugar maples.

Nor do we ream the holes in midseason. No time is available to remove the buckets, pull the spouts, scrape the inside of the holes with the drill bit, and replace the spouts and buckets. So we pass. We rely on the Warner malleable iron spout, whose design, Leader asserts, will control bacteria at the taphole and keep the wretched pests away.

Warner malleable iron sap spouts are part of our sugaring repertoire. They came with the necessaries in 1964. We've used them since the beginning. "Through careful design," the Leader Evaporator Company avers in its *Maple Sugar Makers' Guide*, the Warner spout's taper acts as a dam, seals the hole, and keeps air away. The hole doesn't dry out and heal. Our limited experience with the Warner has not yet validated Leader's claim. The Warner—to us—does not noticeably control bacteria or prevent diminishing sap runs. Though the Warner spout is popular, its popularity comes from its durability and effectiveness in transporting sap, not from the much-acclaimed airtight taper that has little, if any, effect in controlling bacterial access to the taphole. Our 1966 results confirm this. In 1966, I observe shorter and lesser sap runs in the unsanitized tapholes. The presence of air in the taphole costs us sap.

Bacteria require air to access the walls of the taphole. Without air, the annoying microbes cannot do their thing. Plagued by our 1966 production results and Leader's claim, though unfounded, that the Warner spout will seal the hole from air, I reason that a taphole kept full of sap, enough sap—or ice—to plug the access hole day and night, ought not to dry out. A hole full of sap will prevent air—thereby bacterial action—from accessing the walls of the taphole.

In March 1967, Brud, who calls the signals when it's tapping time, is away. I am the decision maker. I tap alone. I don't need to persuade Brud to try the unknown and unproven, cajole him into experimenting with an untried brainstorm to control unseen bacteria. I'll do it myself. I drill the 1967 tapholes slightly downward into the tree, rather than upward, as conventional wisdom has historically dictated. I drill 1,400 holes two inches long down into the xylem, careful not to drill so steep that sap won't make it out over the lip of the spout. I hang the buckets, put on covers, and wait for the sap to come.

At first run the tapholes—and a portion of the spout's channel—flood with sap as I intend, and stay flooded, inaccessible to the bacteria. Sap continues to drip over the ends of the spouts into the buckets as usual. The first run goes well—no lost sap, holes always full. Second run the same. I boil off the syrup and wait for more sap. My partners, of course, think I'm nuts, alleging that the sap is running down the tree trunk. Brud comes home, looks over what I'd done, and is overheard to mutter, "Who the hell tapped these trees?"

"I did," I answer.

"But the sap'll run on the ground," he claims.

"Hasn't yet," I reply.

The sap keeps coming—and coming. Brud thinks it's not going to stop. He boils off ninety-some gallons of syrup from a single day's run. Bill and I keep trucking tankfuls of sap to Day Mountain Road. Brud takes close to twenty hours to get it all boiled off. I stay in Temple sugaring until after the Patriots Day holiday, collecting and boiling sap. It's one of our longest seasons. And we produce a record amount of syrup, 410 gallons, plus what sap we spilled hurrying to empty full buckets and gathering pails into the nine-barrel tank sloshing on the back of the old Chevy truck. A remarkable year, I think, well more than a quart of syrup per taphole, near 40 percent more than any past year.

My experiment is obviously a success. But we won't ever drill our tapholes downward again. Nor will the roadside sugarbush ever again produce four hundred gallons of maple syrup. The following year, 1968, we return to conventional tapping, make limited use of the paraformaldehyde sterilizing pellet, and experience diminished sap yield.

Chapter Ten

A SUGAR MAPLE TOWN

The following year, 1968, we don't take the red Chevy out for its daily exercise until after lunch. Heretofore, we have gathered sap as soon as the temperature goes above freezing. By doing it early, much of what we gather is yesterday's run. Our aim now is to leave time for frozen sap in the buckets to thaw, and new sap to fill up the buckets. We gather it in the afternoon, finish about five o'clock, and boil in the evening. On an average day, we miss supper—or eat it in the saphouse—but we're done by nine o'clock. Our beds are in the village, less than three miles away. We don't miss any sleep.

Our tap count begins to drop. Some landowners ask us to discontinue tapping their trees. We also reduce the number of tapholes in a few of the larger sugar maples. The count drops to less than 1,400. Syrup production drops likewise, down to 325 gallons in 1968. The cost of production is down also, to $5 per gallon, and we salvage a bit of profit out of $2,200 in gross sales. We are comfortable with what we're doing, yet I don't know where we're going.

Evenings bring Temple folks out of their houses. In winters it is the general store where stories are told around the wood heater. Summers it is the baseball field for twilight games with the New Vineyard Yankees and Callahan's Hard Cider Boys. When fall comes, it's hunting stories at the general store again. But in spring it's the saphouse on Day Mountain Road. Folks come to talk—and look around. "Havin' a good season?" they ask. "How much syrup you make in a day?" And invariably they ask, "How many gallons of sap does it take to make a gallon of syrup, anyway?" In the spring our saphouse is the cultural center of Temple, like the Grange or the Good Neighbor Club might be in other seasons. The talk is sugaring.

Temple was born a sugar maple town. Since the time of the first settlers in 1796, Temple has sugared. Perhaps its most notable sugaring period came two hundred years ago in the early 1800s when the homesteaders first came to the hills. Every farmer, finding himself in a hardwood landscape a thousand feet above sea level on rocky glacial till and surrounded by sugar maples, sugared. He had to. He needed sugar in the kitchen, sugar for sweetener, sugar to preserve, and syrup for pancake topping. Temple's homesteaders, as was likely all over Maine, cleared land for farmhouses, barns, and pastures, and saved a small grove of sugar maples near the farmhouse for sugar and syrup production. They likely drilled holes with an old hand-operated bit brace and a carpenter's bit, inserted spiles whittled from sumac or elder or sawn from birch, and hung tin cans—or wooden pails—to catch the sap. Some may have fashioned a flat-bottomed boiling pan from a small piece of sheet metal tacked or nailed to wooden slats to form sides. An arch from stones or bricks enclosed an outdoor fire and supported the pan. Sugaring in Temple's hills and backyards thrives through World Wars I and II and into the twenty-first century.

Cane sugar came to America in the middle 1800s, but not to Temple's hill-farmers. And had it been accessible to the hill-farmers, no respectable Temple farmer would have purchased it. Cane sugar cost too much. A Temple farmer could make his own sugar for less. And Temple farmers supported a widespread boycott against Dominican sugar arising from the use of slave labor in the cane sugar camps. They wouldn't buy cane sugar produced by slaves. Maple sugar remained Maine's primary sweetener until after World War I when cane sugar cost less to buy—on Main Street in most cities—than maple sugar did to make. But not so here in Temple's hills.

With the coming of World War I, cane sugar became scarce and costly again, and America's sugarmakers produced an all-time record American crop of nearly five million gallons of maple syrup, eclipsing the 1860—the coming of the Civil War—record of a bit over four million gallons. This according to the United States Department of Agriculture. Following World War I, however, cane sugar returned in abundant quantities, and maple sugar production began a long decline. By about 1945, maple sugar as a commodity had virtually disappeared, displaced by the cheaper cane sugar, and Maine's maple sugarmakers had turned to maple syrup, promoting it as a topping for pancakes and waffles. In 1950 annual production of syrup in the United States stood at two million gallons—eleven thousand in Maine in 1955—reflecting the shortage then of farm labor. Following 1950, syrup production declined steadily. In 1965, about the time of the coming of Jackson Mountain Maple Farm, Maine produced eight thousand gallons, the lowest in recorded history.

When March 1969 comes, the snow is so deep in Temple I can't find the saphouse. It's hidden behind twelve-foot snowbanks. On March 8, two days before the traditional first sap run, I go to Day Mountain Road to probe for it and clear the path to the front door. The snow is banked over the top of the door. Three of us—Brud, Bill, and me—take all day to shovel a trench to the front door and clear the roof, which is in danger of collapsing. The roof job, which is often push-off work, is worsened by having to throw the snow from the roof upward as high as we can reach to remove it clear of the eave, a once-in-a-lifetime experience for me. The snow-shoveling job requires us to put off tapping for another week until March 15 and 16, just in time for a mid-March freeze-up. The first run, a two-day run near the end of March that requires us to clamber up and down nine-foot snowbanks with full gathering pails again, produces fifty gallons of maple syrup.

April this year is textbook sap weather, clear skies and a twenty-five-degree swing in daily temperatures from 20°F overnight to 45°F midday. Weekdays I drive the Chevy truck—sometimes alone, sometimes with Pa—through Temple's hills collecting sap, visiting, as it were, Temple's past. I'm in awe at what I envision as the ancient doings here. Reminders of the old hill farmers appear out the Chevy's windows, stonewalls along the roadside, apple trees in the forest, a foundation hole, a running-down farmhouse. Occasionally, an old farm is still occupied: the Gallup place one, the Butterfield place another, and the Kennison place, where folks there even now make syrup, perhaps sugar as well, in a home-fashioned flat pan steaming over an arch of cobbles and stones. It's ancient sugaring in real time, as it has been in Temple for a century and a half.

The red Chevy is a dependable horse. Surefooted and relentless, it climbs every hill, navigates every mud hole, and sits patiently at every stop while I scramble over the roadside and fill two sap-gathering pails with sap that I will add to its backbreaking load. It doesn't complain, starts without a whimper, and is agreeable to everything I ask. I couldn't expect a more loyal companion in these hills than the old red Chevy. It takes us—the Chevy and me—an hour to fill the tank and another hour to take the sap to the saphouse and return to the hills. We make the trip about three times a day when the sap runs.

Sap production in 1969 drops to five gallons per taphole, down from the seven or more we've enjoyed the past three years. But the tap count hasn't changed. And the weather, except for the snow, is steady. The snow delays our beginning, of course, and sap doesn't come until late in March. But the season lasts deep into April, about five weeks total, and produces a normal number of days suitable for a sap run. But it's the first significant reduction in syrup production—down to 225 gallons—I've seen from the roadside bush.

Syrup production strengthens a bit the next two years, but in 1972 it dips again, this time to 220 gallons. Tap count is less. Our trees, particularly the oldest and most fragile, are dying. We skip tapping at the hard-to-get-to and dangerous locations, the high banks and slippery slopes. We continue to lose tapholes to landowners who say that continuous tapping is hurting their trees. The decline in taps is small but relentless, falling to less than one thousand tapholes by 1974.

Annual production continues to fall as well, and we start buying syrup. We produce 120 gallons in 1974 and buy fifty, which we blend with our own, regrade and repackage to satisfy the demand for syrup. In 1976 we produce 115 gallons of syrup and buy two fifty-gallon drums to blend with our own. I suspect the presence of bacteria is part of our trouble, trouble that also includes an unbalanced equipment resource caused by the low sap yield. We own too many buckets and too large an evaporator for the sap we collect, which increases the unit cost of production, an expense we are not interested in growing.

Brud leaves in 1973. Our founder and president, now a University of Maine graduate in business, accepts a position with a national insurance company in Milwaukee, Wisconsin. He goes to Milwaukee to train for an executive position. He will return East in 1977, but only as far as Poughkeepsie, New York, where he will purchase a life insurance agency and establish roots. Though he will come to Temple occasionally—seldom during the sap run—he is mainly a source of financial counsel and, should Bill and I be desperate, advice. Presently he is still the principal driver of the company—president, actually, of the corporation—and it's rare that Bill or I would make a significant decision, or change how we operate, without his counsel. But he is constructively gone.

And come 1977, our equipment goes weary. The Chevy truck, nearly twenty years old now, is used up, rusty, the battery weak, its brakes suspected to be inadequate. The suction pump we use to transfer sap from roadside barrels to the nine-barrel tank on the Chevy's back disappears, stolen. And we—Bill and I—grow weary of climbing snowbanks, sap slopping out of a half-full gathering pail. And the saphouse, the remnant of several abandoned buildings along Day Mountain Road that Brud dismantled and resurrected fifteen years ago, is collapsing under the weight of twelve Maine winters, the roof damaged and leaking and the structure pushed three feet off its posts by the oppressive snow. In 1978 I sense a new technology coming that will leave us behind. It's time to move, again. We need a new place, a place of our own. I talk to Brud. He agrees.

Chapter Eleven

WE OWN A FARM

IN 1978 BRUD COMES TO TEMPLE FROM POUGHKEEPSIE TO RESCUE HIS sugaring business. He agrees that tapping the roadside is no longer an option. It's unproductive. It's inefficient. To bring the bush back to full production is impossible. Tapping roadside sugar maples that we don't own is unpopular. And bacteria are seemingly uncontrollable. He agrees we should abandon the roadside, come up with a new idea, and build a new system, preferably on a site favorable to the use of plastic tubing.

We scout the town for a grove of sugar maples on sloping land we can buy. We look mainly on roads we've been tapping, places where sap will run to the road, a grove, say, that will support the capacity of our existing evaporator, storage tank, and filter. Sugar maples are not hard to find in Temple. They're everywhere. But in the quantity and size tree we seek, we find little that is accessible by road. Much of Temple was cleared in the 1800s for development—that is, hill-farming, or has been logged during the past fifty years, rendering many sugar maples too small. We find sugar maples that are unavailable; we find sugar maples that are inaccessible; we find sugar maples on sites unfavorable to a gravity gathering system. And then we find a piece of land that looks possible to sugar on—and it's for sale. The land, one hundred acres of northern mixed hardwood forest, sits next to Orchard Hill Road about one mile west of Temple village and is presently being sliced up into residential lots. It's on land likely once part of my great grandfather William Hodgkins's hill-farm. Brud and I go for a hike.

The land slopes to the southeast and Orchard Hill Road. A forested hillside, it comprises young sugar maples, beech, ash, and birch. Sap will flow by gravity to the road from anyplace on the land. Electricity is accessible on Orchard Hill Road within one thousand feet. A nearby roadside spring of potable water is popular with the public. We like it.

William Hodgkins was our great grandfather. Born in Temple in 1834, he married twenty-year-old Mary Locklin in 1856. After thirty-something years of farming with his father, Alpheus, in the northern part of Temple, he acquired land on Orchard Hill in 1874, the Zadok Smith place, and moved there with Mary. He soon acquired the nearby Lewis Libby farm and the greater part of the Warren Farmer place and merged the three farms, comprising two hundred acres at the intersection of what is now Varnum and Orchard Hill roads, into one. Over the next thirty-five years, William raised prize-winning cattle, tended flocks of sheep, and grew apples, orchards of Spice and Baldwin that in a decent year yielded two hundred barrels for the flourishing apple market. And he produced maple sugar and syrup from his sugar maples for use in Mary's kitchen.

William died in 1911 at age seventy-seven, the result of a conflagration with one of his oxen. His oldest son, Sheriden, whom I knew and, as a nine-year-old, helped hay his fields during World War II for $1 a day, inherited William's farm and managed it until his death in 1952. Following Sheriden's death, farming ceased on the two hundred acres, and the land, cleared for settlement in the early 1800s, was allowed to restore to its original forested condition.

Notwithstanding the land's history, the sugar maples alone appeal to me. The one hundred acres of William's hill farm, the now Temple Oaks Subdivision, is owned by East Wilton land developer Moonstone Incorporated. Moonstone has exploited its attractive location by creating a number of sizable house lots offering privacy and opportunity for country living. Old stone walls wind through the forest and offer a bit of historic ambiance as well. Eighteen residential sites exist; all are offered for sale. Brud and I, carrying a lot plan with us, traipse up and down over three contiguous sizeable lots and estimate 1,500 sugar maples of at least twelve-inches diameter chest high. A few at the top of Orchard Hill are as chesty even at twenty-four inches diameter. The three lots are unsold. "Buy 'em," Brud says. I agree, and we buy the three lots, about thirty acres according to Moonstone's plan. We own a farm. It's 1975.

I plan the development of the site. First, a sturdy and spacious sap-house, one that will stand on its own feet, one that we can keep clean, one with space for filtering, heating, and canning finished syrup, and a counter to work on. The saphouse also will include a concrete floor, electricity for lights and pumps, water for washing, and an out-the-saphouse-door access to the sugarbush. Using stiff paper, I build a scale-down model of the saphouse such that Brud and Bill can espy the relative dimensions.

I sketch a network of plastic tubing for Orchard Hill. I'm confident plastic tubing will work well on the steep slopes there and will eliminate the onerous and expensive labor of gathering sap. Advocates of plastic tubing tell me, too, that plastic tubing will deliver more sap. Cleaner sap, also. Gathering sap with gathering pails is over. Our galvanized sap buckets, once we leave Day Mountain Road, will be abandoned and likely gather dust and cobwebs in a barn someplace.

Plastic tubing for sap collection first appeared in Maine in 1959. Warren Voter, an agent for various maple syrup equipment manufacturers who will sell Jackson Mountain Maple Farm three thousand galvanized buckets five years later, demonstrated the use of plastic tubing at his sugarbush on Voter Hill in West Farmington and promoted its use. Before then, before the coming of plastic tubing to Maine, as far back as the turn of the century, only a few Maine producers had experimented with pipelines—metal or wood troughs or metal pipes—to convey sap. But the early-day pipelines did not measure up. Pipes froze and burst; troughs sagged; sap overflowed and was lost; vapor locks plugged flow in the pipelines; and wooden troughs and metal pipes proved too difficult to clean.

The onerous cost of time collecting sap tree to tree—usually on foot—was not eliminated either by the early pipelines. Gathering sap tree to tree was still necessary. And in addition, workers carried the sap on foot for some distance to nearby collection points where they dumped it into barrels. The barrels then fed it through another crude pipeline to the saphouse. Rarely, if ever, before Voter's introduction of revolutionary plastic tubing in 1959, had a system of gravity sap collection from taphole to saphouse been effectively used in Maine. Pipelines had proved unfit for sugaring's future.

Voter, confident that he had struck upon the future of sap gathering and collecting, proclaimed his revolutionary plastic pipeline system superior. Though plastic required a one-time financial investment about equal to the bucket and cover setup, Voter was convinced that plastic tubes promised elimination of costly labor. It would not be necessary to touch the sap with human hands. The system also, Voter alleged, increased sap production. Sap would no longer be slopped or sloshed or spilled out of gathering pails, diluted with rain and snow, lost out the bottom of leaky buckets, or flow over the top of full ones.

Voter knew how to run the plastic lines. He kept them off the ground, well up into the sun-warmed air where frozen sap thawed quickly on cold mornings, allowing a full sap flow. He strung his lines early in the season, before the first run, and was ready when the sap showed up. He protected his lines from animals—deer and moose—grazing in his bush by leaving a loop of slack in the line at each tree. Maine's maple producers, Voter predicted, would all convert to the superior plastic tubes.

Two years later, however, Voter, who at that time was a member of the fledgling Maine Maple Producers Association, reported that perhaps 20 percent of Maine's producers had converted to the meandering tube. Conversion, he reported, had been slowed by troublesome experiences. Vapor locks in mainlines and laterals had blocked the flow of sap; producers, unsure whether to use vented or unvented lines, experimented with each and suffered poor results with both. Though Voter had previously related that producers could anticipate high pressures in the tree that would force sap through the tubing, high tree pressures did not occur. And in many cases, producers were forced to relocate sap lines to establish sufficient force to overcome vapor locks and carry sap toward the saphouse. In other cases, particularly in mainlines located on level ground, producers needed to install pumps to move the sap.

Effective methods of cleaning tubing were not available then either. Most producers faced the onerous task of taking the tubing down, pumping water through it, drying it, storing it, and then putting it up again in the same place the following year, a virtually impossible task without a tubing-network map coded to locations in the bush where the tubing lines fit the trees. Because of such unanticipated and nagging problems, producers in the early days of tubing limited its use to steep hillsides and other isolated hard-to-access sites, and delayed implementing its widespread use.

In 1976, the year following the purchase of our Orchard Hill farm and before we are ready to move there, I install a few short tubing lines, maybe thirty tapholes, on the lower slopes of Orchard Hill, and connect the lines to a half-inch black plastic water pipe running to a roadside tank. From the tank, I pump the sap onto the Chevy truck for the trip to the Day Mountain Road saphouse. This unvented setup shows me firsthand that sap collection by plastic tubing is plausible.

In 1978, two years later, I notice plastic tubing has acquired status in many other Maine sugarbushes. It's becoming an efficient and effective collection scheme, and has attracted workshops and demonstrations and lectures for the benefit of producers. Chester Basford, Benton producer, invites Vermont tubing specialist Lew Bissell to put on a technical tubing demonstration at Basford's farm, where producers come and learn the latest installation techniques. Stevens and Bates, a maple syrup producer in Carroll, Maine, puts up more than seven thousand feet of plastic tubing, and reports it working "without a hitch."

As plastic tubing appears in Maine's sugarbushes and along Maine's roadside stonewalls, galvanized buckets fade from view, particularly in sloping groves. In backyards and on front lawns, I see tubing running into five-gallon plastic pails sitting on the ground, rather than a bucket hooked to a spout or nailed to a tree. And the introduction of pumping stations in the collection system, which producers are inclined to do, broadens the use of tubing to flat land. Plastic tubing is here, and the advantages are numerous and visible: more sap, no spillage, and clean lines strung taut without sags. Air is barred from access to tapholes, decreasing bacterial activity. Backwashing the lines at the end of the season produces cleaner sap the following year. By 1979, it seems that plastic tubing lines are the gathering system of choice in Maine sugarbushes.

ORCHARD HILL ROAD

IN 1978 HARTLEY FARMER, DESCENDENT OF THE HEADY HILL-FARMING days in Temple's hills and local building contractor managing our sugaring development, comes to Orchard Hill Road to start the project. He prepares our saphouse site for placement of a twenty-by-thirty-two-foot rectangular concrete slab, back a bit from the road and handy to a nearby spring. Later, when the concrete has hardened, he frames our saphouse with new lumber and vents the interior through the roof with a cupola, the cupola doors movable from the inside by ropes and pulleys. The five-foot-by-fourteen-foot Leader Special, trucked from Day Mountain Road on the back of the red Chevy truck—perhaps the final piece of farmwork for the unregistered Chevy—fits nicely through the double front doors, and we place it on the concrete a tad off-center, favoring the hillside and the back door. Farmer erects a countertop along the roadside wall and leaves space in the front of the building for a table and chairs should we choose to entertain guests. And he builds an enclosed platform against the outside wall—the uphill side—for a storage tank.

I request electric service from Central Maine Power Company. I learn that a power line does not currently exist within one thousand feet of my location on Orchard Hill Road, so I will be required to sign a minimum-use agreement. I don't know how much electricity costs or how much of it I will use monthly, but at this point I don't really care. I sign a five-year agreement for $15 per month. Time will show, I believe, that I have done it right. A Central Maine Power Company line crew shows up the next day and goes to work on the line extension. Before a year is up, a residence will appear on Orchard Hill Road and connect into the line extension; the power company will negate my minimum-use agreement and install a meter at my place. Meanwhile, I switch my attention to Orchard Hill and what will be our sugarbush.

Brud decides we should thin the forest a bit, expose the trees to more sky and provide space for the sugar maples to expand their crowns. I agree. I know that settlers created their own small sugarbushes by selective cutting a piece of their quarter sections. They culled all species of trees—oak, beech, ash, hemlock, et al.—except the sugar maples. They left the sugar maples to thrive and grow more leaves, increasing sugar levels. They used the brush, tops, and waste wood for firewood and the sawlogs for flooring and furniture. We intend much of the same. We hire a cutter. He drags the cuttings with a dozer to the front yard of the saphouse. We sell the culls for firewood. For three years we thin in the summer and fall when the tubing is down. After three years we have done enough.

Also in 1978, we choose to install a plastic tubing network as our primary sap-collection system on Orchard Hill, a choice based less on what my associates and neighboring producers are doing than on my own experience with plastic tubing. My experiment with thirty tapholes in our new bush and boiling off the sap on Day Mountain Road is now two years old, and my observations there convince me to use tubing on the entire hill. I observe that sap yields are higher in the tubing setup, mainly, I reason, because the steeper slope produces what is termed a natural vacuum in full lines, which pulls the sap downslope out of the tapholes. The unvented tubing, I also observe, seals the tapholes from intruding air, keeps the tapholes wet, and will, I expect, eliminate or slow the consequent growth of bacteria and healing of the taphole walls during the sugaring season. And the tight-tubed system eliminates spillage, too. No spillage guarantees more sap.

I put together a plan for the plastic network. Three-quarter-inch black plastic water pipe will form the mainline, which will run roughly up the southeasterly property line—the land slopes to the southeast— toward the top of Orchard Hill. Three-quarter-inch laterals connected to the mainline will run uphill toward the northwesterly property line, accessing the sugar maples. I will suspend the mainline and laterals above ground, tie the lines to trees, and apply tension with tiebacks.

Five-sixteenths-inch plastic tubing will run downslope, tree to tree, as close to the fall line as possible to induce natural vacuum in the sap lines. Lines running full are expected to create a slight negative pressure at the taphole and draw more sap from the hole. It's an unintended consequence of using plastic tubing. Not even Warren Voter, the first champion of plastic tubing in Maine, anticipated the tubing to create its own vacuum.

I will limit individual tubing lines to forty taps, less than the cap of sixty suggested to us. We intend to take the tubing down every spring and wash it. So I limit the weight of individual lines to what I can carry up the hill, thus the forty-tap maximum. To access tapholes beyond the forty, I will extend an existing lateral.

I am attracted to the idea of mechanically induced vacuum in the lines. The progressive producers in Maine—Ted Greene, who sugars in East Sebago and was the first to set up a small network of Maple-Flo tubing; Arnold Luce, the first to install a reverse osmosis sap filter; Jeremy Steeves; Chester Basford; and more—are all talking vacuum pumps. I am beguiled by the thought of sap traveling on its own all the way to the storage tank simply because the producer extracted the air from the lines.

Equipment dealers are hyping vacuum also. Leader Evaporator Company's 1961 *Maple Sugar Makers' Guide* suggests vacuum be used to supplement falling tree pressures near the end of a sap run. In their 1975 catalog, however, Leader advertises vacuum pumps for sale and reports that vacuum in the lines "does the job quite well." And a vacuum pump, it's said by some, will increase sap yields 50 percent. It will keep lines clean, prevent ice blockage from forming overnight, and provide considerable negative pressure at the taphole on lowry days. Vacuum talk in the 1970s is upbeat. By all accounts vacuum will compensate us— and more—for the low sugar content sap in our pole trees, which grow thirty-five feet straight up before the tops can produce a few leaves. I look around for a vacuum pump.

I call Wes Kinney. Kinney is a former teacher at North Yarmouth Academy whom I inspired a few years ago to give sugaring a try. He opened a sugarbush in Auburn and kept it producing until he bought a dairy farm on Knox Ridge. Kinney's a Knox dairy farmer now, planning to develop a sugarbush on his land there. He tells me he has a vacuum pump, "A one-hundred-year-old DeLavel sitting in a corner of my barn. Found it here, hasn't been used for years," he says. To me, it's state of the art, and he gives it to me. Wes brings it to Orchard Hill, and we lift the iron monstrosity off the back of his pickup truck onto my saphouse floor. "Give it plenty of oil," he says, as though he's instructing me on how to feed a horse, "and it will treat you right."

I need a releaser to go with the vacuum pump. I have vacuum in the lines now that will draw sap to the saphouse, but I need to somehow release the sap into the storage tank without losing any vacuum in the lines. I find a releaser—actually a contraption—in Leader's catalog, a sap extractor it's called, made by the Universal Milking Machine Company, the same company that manufactured Wes's vacuum pump a hundred years ago. I buy it. It comes to Temple in a box. It's in pieces, maybe a hundred pieces. Directions for assembly are included, something like the model railroad setup I bought my kids last Christmas.

PARAFORMALDEHYDE

I DECIDE NOT TO USE THE PARAFORMALDEHYDE STERILIZING PELLET ON Orchard Hill. I give up on it. I'm convinced the pill will damage and eventually kill the young sugar maples. My primary evidence comes from the few pelletized tapholes on Orchard Hill I've bored the past two years. After two years they aren't healing. Vertical columns of discolored and decayed xylem—sapwood—extend above and below the tapholes. Sapwood there is dead or dying, suffering from the pellet. Decay in the vicinity of the taphole is extensive, perhaps an inch and a half above and below and a half inch either side, likely more damage than when settlers tapped a tree by slashing it with a hatchet. From what I can see of the few tapholes I've experimented with, sapwood growth is stunted and likely won't overcome the decay. The trees will run out of live xylem in only a few years. Then they'll die.

I reason there is no need to sterilize the taphole anyway. A closed tubing network, tapered plastic spouts, and vacuum in the lines will curb the presence of bacteria; the unvented tubing system will block the pesky microbes virtually as effectively as the pellet. And should a microbe happen to squeeze into a taphole somehow, it will be immediately sucked out by the vacuum pump. Brud and Bill agree. Twelve years later, the Maine Department of Agriculture will follow my lead and ban use of the controversial sterilizing pellets in sugar maple tapholes statewide.

The paraformaldehyde sterilizing pellet was developed in 1962 by researcher R. N. Costilow at Michigan State University. Costilow's research sought a germicide that would free tapholes of harmful—what sugarmakers considered harmful—microorganisms. Producers had complained for years of the onerous task of reaming tapholes midway through the sugaring season to maintain sap flow. Their choices had been few: ream the hole or not ream the hole. Those who reamed maintained normal sap flow throughout a season. Those who didn't ream suffered large reductions in sap yield. Richard Eaton, for example, a four-thousand-tap producer in East Corinth, wrote in a 1946 letter to Ken Cooper, secretary of the MMPA, that failure to ream had cost him a third of his crop, more than three hundred gallons of maple syrup.

Costilow's research resulted in development of a 250 mg paraformaldehyde pellet, a solid form of the liquid disinfectant formaldehyde, suitable for inserting into a taphole prior to inserting a spout. In experiments conducted by Costilow, 250 mg of paraformaldehyde effectively sterilized the interior surfaces of the hole for a typical six-week sugaring season, offering producers an alternate choice—a dose of paraformaldehyde—to maintain sap flow the entire season.

Costilow also claimed to have determined the pellet to be safe. The residual level of paraformaldehyde in maple syrup produced from sterilized tapholes measured, in experiments conducted by Costilow, less than two parts per million, within the tolerance level set by the United States Food and Drug Administration and Health and Welfare Canada in 1965. Based on Costilow's work, the United States Food and Drug Administration and Health Welfare Canada approved the use of the 250 mg paraformaldehyde pellet as a taphole sterilizer without further research. Maple producers, in search of a convenient way to sustain high sap yields, were attracted to the pellet immediately and, once they had used it, spoke favorably of its effect on sap yields, particularly during warmer weather. Warren Voter, agent for maple equipment and supplies in Franklin County, Maine, reported eighty-five thousand pellets sold in 1965. That seemed to solve the issue.

Scientists and environmentalists in Vermont and elsewhere, however, balked at the pellet's use, concerned that the paraformaldehyde caused excessive decay in the tree beyond just the taphole. The sterilizer, they alleged, constrained the development of healthy sapwood—xylem—sufficiently to warrant discontinuing its use. Mariafranco Morselli, professor and research director at the University of Vermont Department of Botany, following a lengthy review of contemporary research of the pellet's effects on sugar maple xylem, concluded that paraformaldehyde was a threat to sugar maple health. The pellet, she avowed, threatened tree survival itself.

Later in 1970, additional research on trees in Vermont, New York, Michigan, Maine, and Pennsylvania showed extensive vertical columns of discolored and decayed xylem wood, longer and wider than observed in untreated tapholes, clear evidence that paraformaldehyde-treated tapholes fostered the invasion of wood-decaying fungi. Later research in Wisconsin confirmed the earlier results. Morselli, upon conclusion of an extensive review of the environmental risks of paraformaldehyde in sugar maple tapholes, recommended the pellet be discontinued and banned. In 1982 the state of Vermont declared the pellet an unregistered and illegal pesticide. In 1991 the United States Food and Drug Administration and Health and Welfare Canada deemed the pellet an unregistered pesticide as well, and denied registration. Following counseling by the North American Maple Syrup Council (NAMSC) and the International Maple Syrup Institute (IMSI), the United States Food and Drug Administration and Health Welfare Canada declared the pellet illegal everywhere, including Maine.

Not all producers, however, stopped using the pellet. Too much was at stake to summarily reduce sap yields. Following the 1994 season, Morselli alleged that the manufacture of the pellet continued and that as many as three million or more pellets may have been used during both the 1993 and 1994 sap seasons. The matter of tree health had obviously not been resolved.

In 2001 Leon Graves, commissioner of the Vermont Department of Agriculture, stepped into the controversy. Graves wrote Lyle Vanclief, Canadian Minister of Agriculture, expressing concern over unsubstantiated, but repeated, allegations that "paraformaldehyde pellets are in wide use in Quebec." In response to the letter, Vanclief ordered a survey. The survey, an on-site review of physical evidence, indicated that twenty-five of the fifty surveyed Quebecois sugarbushes still used the paraformalde-hyde pellet. Such evidence in Maine, however, was lacking. We at Jackson Mountain Maple Farm, for one, had actually stopped using the pellet of our own accord in 1979.

In 1979 on Orchard Hill, sugar maples are free from exposure to para-formaldehyde—and bacteria as well. The tubing network is unvented, the lines are sealed, air cannot access the system. Unvented tubing is the first line of defense against taphole contamination. Vacuum is preventing all deleterious forms of life, including the blasted microbe, from accessing the taphole. I am convinced that the absence of air inside the tubing is the answer to the bacteria issue, and I turn my attention to being ready to boil sap when it comes.

The second matter we clarify before we boil any sap on Orchard Hill is fuel. We will not fire the evaporator with wood on Orchard Hill Road. Though the saphouse sits midst some thirty acres of hardwood forest, for-est that continually yearns for thinning to make room for the emergence of sugar maple crowns, we switch to heating oil as our primary fuel. Fuel oil makes sense to us, economic sense and social sense. Brud acquires two used oil burners and mounts both of them on the front of the big Leader Special. Hartley Farmer sets two fuel tanks against the outside wall of the saphouse and runs an oil line to the burners.

Using fuel oil to fire a maple syrup evaporator is not unheard of in 1979 in Maine. But it is rare. Though oil-fired evaporators date back to midcentury—the 1950s—few sugarmakers experiment with their use. Though producers see a great convenience in oil-fired evaporators, oil burners are seen as inefficient and costly. Consequently, most producers stay away from fuel oil. Luce's Maple Farm in Anson, however, is an exception. Luce, who is said to use fuel oil routinely, has burned fuel oil in his firebox since 1963 or so, when the price was about fifteen cents per gallon. And it's said that Raymond Titcomb on Titcomb Hill in Farm-ington uses a bit of waste motor oil, squirting a small amount into his firebox occasionally to energize his wood and stabilize his fire. So using fuel oil to fire an evaporator is not a new idea. But it's not popular with Maine maple producers either, not in 1979.

In 1979 fuel oil is virtually unavailable to a maple producer, a result of the most serious national energy shortage in the nation's history. The shortage, largely the result of embargoed oil imports, turns the nation into turmoil. President Nixon appears on television, directs citizens to comply with a national voluntary speed limit of fifty miles per hour, and to turn down thermostats in their homes, all to reduce the use of the nation's fuel stocks. Gasoline stations limit customers to five-gallon purchases, and lines extend from the pump out into the street and around the block. Suburbanites scramble for wood to supplement home heating oil. Oil-fired energy plants convert to coal. And the price per gallon of fuel oil rockets to $1.30, up from fifteen cents just a few short years ago. Yet Jackson Mountain Maple Farm agrees to the price of $1.30 per gallon, eliminates the saphouse woodpile, and installs two oil burners on the front of its big Leader Special to fire the arch, a bold move, particularly in the face of the president's entreaty for sacrifice.

Why? We are working people. We have jobs and growing families. We have no time to cut, stack, and restack eight cords of firewood every summer and fall. And our saphouse is accessible to an oil delivery truck. Yes, we know that buying oil is costly. Our first tankful costs us $350. But so is firewood costly. At $130 per cord for firewood, I figure fuel oil costs us about the same per British Thermal Unit (BTU)—the amount of heat required to produce a unit of work—as firewood. The number of BTUs required is the same. It takes 0.04 cords of wood at $130 per cord, or four gallons of fuel oil at $1.30 per gallon to produce a gallon of maple syrup. The cost to us is the same either way, $5.20 per gallon. We switch to fuel oil.

Ironically, at the same time—the time of turn-down-the-thermostat and all that—I install a parlor wood burner in my home in suburban Yarmouth. With the thermostat down and bedrooms denied of any direct heating at all, I need a warm spot in the house, a place that folks coming in from the cold can sidle up to, or where we can sit and talk and watch television on a cold evening. I figure we're better off in both places, burning wood at home and fuel oil in the saphouse.

CHAPTER FOURTEEN

PLASTIC TUBING RESCUES
MAINE'S MAPLE SYRUP INDUSTRY

IN THE SPRING OF 1979, WE ARE READY TO TAP ORCHARD HILL.
Beguiled by the promise of an early spell of warm weather, we challenge
The Old Farmer's Almanac and tap in February. We work on snowshoes,
carry rolls of tubing up the hill, and string it from tree to tree. We select
healthy-looking trees greater than ten inches in diameter and bore seven-
sixteenths-inch diameter holes into the xylem. We bore shallow, less than
two inches. The xylem is thin in the young trees, and we are careful not
to bore into the heartwood for fear we will lose sap—and vacuum, as
well—into the interior. We connect each taphole to a tubing line via an
unvented plastic spout inserted firmly into the xylem, an eighteen-inch
dropline, and a five-sixteenths-inch diameter tee. The tubing lines run
to three-quarter-inch lateral lines and mainlines that will carry the sap
downhill to our storage tank. We finish the network to near the top of
Orchard Hill, 1,200 taps, perhaps five miles of plastic tubing, before the
first sap run and leave the top of the hill for another year. I need to put
vacuum into the lines we have in place.

Universal's sap extractor is almost beyond words. It is complex, an
assemblage of pieces: dispenser jars, valves, tubing, pulsaters, buffers,
hoses, and clamps that when assembled will connect two flapper valves
whose function is to alternately release sap to the storage tank. When
I have the contraption assembled—three hours later—I learn that I'm

blocked from setting it in place over the tank. It doesn't fit under the storage shed roof. So I cut a hole in the roof, lower the extractor through the hole, mount it over the tank, and connect the assembled composition of metal and plastic and tubing and valves to the vacuum on one side and to the three-quarter-inch mainline pipe coming out of the sugarbush on the other. When done, I flick a switch and watch vacuum build in the system to where my gauge reads 15 inHg, as much as the old horse is likely able to produce. Maximum attainable vacuum at sea level is one Atmosphere, 30 inHg. I'm satisfied with 15 inHg.

The sap comes on March 19 when a decent run fills the storage tank. At a vacuum level of 15 inHg, sap is drawn from the lines to one of the two dispenser jars. Every few seconds, as a dispenser jar fills, vacuum—and sap flow—is automatically switched to the alternate jar. A gravity-activated flapper valve then opens under the first jar, and sap drops into the storage tank, all while maintaining 15 inHg vacuum in the sap lines. For me, it's an amazing contrivance of anomalous pieces joined together with a myriad of eyebolts and wing nuts, similar to something one might see on a launch pad at Cape Canaveral. The vacuum guarantees a continuous negative pressure at the taphole; the tree doesn't know—or care—where it comes from. A steady run of sap—"All from our own trees," Beth exclaims, "first time in history"—flows into the extractor, where a cumulation of it drops into the storage tank every few seconds, oblivious to how it arrives there. I call it a tree-to-tank gathering and collecting system.

Now that it is up and in place, I admire our new tree-to-tank gathering setup. The shiny lines hover in place, suspended, poised, and ready for the transport of sap a quarter-mile and more to the storage tank at the saphouse. Until now a sap run has been a full day's work for two people emptying buckets all day, and then a tedious late-night effort to turn the run into syrup, extinguish the fire—no small task, either—and package the syrup in pretty lithographed cans. Now, if we've done it right, we'll go to the saphouse around four-thirty in the afternoon, light the fire with the flick of a switch, put it out ninety minutes later with another flick, package the syrup, and then go home for a seven o'clock supper.

The first sap run, which lasts one day, produces fifteen gallons of maple syrup. The season, the first on Orchard Hill, ends in mid-April and nets us 215 gallons of syrup in four weeks. I breathe a sigh. Sap yield is up; syrup production is restored.

Maine has never been a major producer of maple syrup. Of the top ten maple-producing states in 1926, the earliest ranking recorded by Willits, Maine placed ninth. During the years following 1926, when cane sugar was being introduced into the American market, commercial sugaring in Maine held steady at just about eight thousand gallons per year, consistently ninth or tenth among the top ten states. In 1964, when Jackson Mountain Maple Farm started producing, Maine still produced eight thousand gallons annually, but it had fallen out of the top ten syrup-producing states, behind Minnesota. By 1971 Minnesota had dropped back, and Maine, still at eight thousand gallons, was ninth again. But in 1979, as plastic tubing and vacuum began its widespread implementation in Maine, syrup production edged upward. Maine produced nine thousand gallons that year, yet remained in ninth place.

Until effective plastic tubing and applied vacuum came to Maine, a producer was limited in the size of his sugarbush. He could do only so much work in a day, and if sap ran every day into buckets, he was restricted, depending on his means of gathering sap and the size of his labor force, to as few as three thousand tapholes, perhaps five thousand in some circumstances, and be able to get all the work of gathering and boiling done in a day. A part-time producer—farmer—could handle perhaps three thousand buckets in a day; producers with ample labor—a large family—and ample equipment might tap five thousand. Maine's growth in syrup production was constrained by what was possible. A producer, no matter the number of sugar maples within his resources, could not tap enough to earn a living exclusively from sugaring. It was impossible. Maine in 1979—in 1926 as well—had likely reached its taphole limit. The coming of plastic tubing and applied vacuum, however, removed the tapping barrier. And in 1979 the future of Maine sugaring looked brighter.

Maine producers, buoyed by their newfound prospects, turned unrestrained to plastic tubing and vacuum. Though the transition from buckets was slow, the results were good. Plastic tubing in sugarbushes moved toward general use. Sap yields increased. Profits too, and interest in sugaring swelled. Producers added tapholes, expanded their sugarbushes, and opened up new areas. They were no longer constrained by galvanized buckets, a dray, and a tractor.

During the 1980s, plastic tubing networks, augmented by vacuum, clearly demonstrated an ability to produce a greater amount of sap. Sap yields increased to new levels, as much as ten gallons per taphole, and more, in a forested bush. Syrup production also. A quart of syrup per taphole was reachable. And the number of tapholes kept growing, up to as many as twenty-five thousand in a single sugarbush. Some called the decade of the 1980s the plastic revolution. In 1989, at the end of the decade, Maine producers reported 103,000 gallons of syrup produced, up from 76,000 gallons the year before and 10,000 gallons in 1984. Plastic networks—gravity gathering systems—had outperformed buckets by an incalculable amount. The adoption of a gravity gathering system, which required virtually no crew time, was seen by many as the most significant change ever in the history of maple sugaring. In Maine, it rescued the industry. As one producer was heard to say, plastic tubing "provided an image for the twenty-first century that was not born in the eighteenth."

The plastic revolution in Maine actually dated back to 1959 when Warren Voter put up a plastic tubing demonstration at his sugarbush in West Farmington. Voter's demonstration was likely the first hint that sugaring as we had known it, grown up with, and practiced, would ultimately disappear. Though the change started slowly and many Maine producers were generally skeptical at first, it grew exponentially and, as the 1980s came to a close, the results of Maine's search for an effective and profitable technique for sap gathering were evident to anyone aware of the production statistics.

In 1981 Jackson Mountain Maple Farm completes its own transition to plastic tubing and applied vacuum. We tap the entire thirty-acre network on Orchard Hill for the first time, 1,500 tapholes interconnected with five miles of plastic tubing.

Warm weather in the winter of 1981 causes us, once again, to challenge *The Old Farmer's Almanac*, which characteristically predicts the first sap run for March 10. We tap in February and we win. First run comes on March 1. It's a prodigious run. "The sap is just pouring out," Beth exclaims. "I've never seen it run like this, not ever." The sap runs for three days, stopping for a time at night to recharge. Bill and I boil and bottle nonstop except to sleep a bit. After three days we have sixty-five gallons of maple syrup. We finish boiling sap on March 28, one of the shortest seasons in our history, twenty-eight days. We produce 315 gallons of maple syrup, a bumper crop of pole-tree sap, an amount per taphole exceeded only in 1967 when I kept the roadside tapholes flooded with sap. We bottle it for sale in consumer-sized plastic containers, a change from the metal containers we have used since 1964 and a continuation of the industry's transition to plastic.

The 1981 season on Orchard Hill convinces me that the plastic revolution is real. It has reached Jackson Mountain Maple Farm. Sap yield reaches near nine gallons per taphole. The storage tank fills on a single sap run. No sap drips on the ground through leaky buckets. No sap sloshes out of gathering pails or spills as it did when I lifted it into the tank on the old red Chevy truck. Sap runs into the evenings—or all night. Sap is clean—no floating moths, no dead mice—and the boiling syrup looks lighter. Syrup production is up, too. And we have more money in the bank.

We jettison our past. We sell the Day Mountain Road saphouse to a Farmington sport looking for a hunting camp. The old red Chevy truck retires to the yard of its former owner. We upend its three-hundred-gallon gathering tank in front of the saphouse as an inducement to a possible buyer—or perhaps as lawn art. We sell—and give away—buckets and malleable iron spouts to all comers. The bucket washer, adjustable rotating scrub brushes mounted in a galvanized tank supported at working height on a metal frame that will, according to the Leader Company, wash buckets fast and efficiently, is sold to a small producer in Knox, who obviously is not heeding the plastic revolution. We are free from the bondage of 1960s sugaring.

Demand for our syrup is up, as is interest in our sugaring setup. Folks driving by the saphouse on Orchard Hill Road—possibly three or four cars each day—wave. Art Mitchell, a classmate in the Temple Village School in the 1940s and a teammate on the Temple Townies baseball team in the 1950s, comes in to look at what's happening here. "How far up the hill do your lines run?"

"About a half-mile," I tell him.

"So how do you wash them? All stretched out a half mile like that?"

"We carry them down here to the saphouse and pump water through."

Most folks come to see us when steam is floating upward out of the cupola. They come inside, watch sap bubble and boil and flow through the Leader Special, and maybe ask a question or two. "How many gallons of sap does it take, anyway, to make a gallon of syrup?" Some buy a quart or even two. Some don't. We read about ourselves in *The Franklin Journal*. *The Waterville Sentinel* publishes a photo essay of what we're doing here. People talk about us in the coffee shops. Retailers want our syrup.

"YOUR SYRUP SELLS GREAT"

WHEN 1982 COMES, JACKSON MOUNTAIN FARM IS ON SOLID FOOTING. We are independent, in control, and owners of a licensed syrup-making enterprise producing three hundred gallons of Maine maple syrup annually on our own land. By all evidence, our future is bright. The bush is organized; sap yields are up. Bacteria, it seems, are under control. Our maple syrup is popular and in demand, our sales potential seemingly constrained only by the amount of syrup we can produce. Yet though the company is intact and sound, the three partners, the founders, are scattered.

Brud has been absent the longest. He left syrup making in 1973 and went to the city—Milwaukee, Wisconsin—where his footing was, so to speak. Though in 1977, he returned to the East as far as Poughkeepsie, New York, and keeps in touch with Bill and me; he comes to Temple only when he can scratch out a bit of time, and seldom during the sugaring season. Bill and I miss him.

Bill left sugaring in 1975 for the University of Maine graduate school, seeking a place for himself in the business world. He found it one year later, 1976, when he managed the Hodgkins General Store in Temple a month for his ill dad. "I really like it here," he told a newspaper reporter at the time. "I get a kick out of it." He purchased the store from his father later that year and hunkered down in Temple. Though he continued to participate in syrup production and marketing, by 1982 his sugaring interests are overrun by the needs of the general store and his busy young family. He focuses on participating in his kids' activities—a baseball Dad, one might say—and wringing enough net earnings out of the ancient—1895—general store to support his family. Producing maple syrup is not part of his equation. He has learned, of course, during the past eighteen or so years, as we all have, that money to live on and raise a family is not to be found manufacturing maple syrup. So Bill necessarily limits his Jackson Mountain Farm commitment to the absolutely necessary, boiling sap when it runs.

I am in the same category. In 1982 my youngsters are all in high school in Yarmouth and require significant time and attention. And I now hold two, sometimes three, jobs: the engineering job with the transportation agency, which is now a management job; a private engineering consultant job Saturdays and evenings; and a sales job as agent for various maple syrup supply vendors, including the Leader Evaporator Company and the Bacon Jug Company. During the sap run in March, I alternate nights sleeping at home in Yarmouth and at Bill's in Temple. Occasionally, when circumstances permit—or demand—I take a deep breath and reflect a bit on where I'm headed. Then I go back to one of the three jobs. Right now, Jackson Mountain Farm has a profuse amount of maple syrup in inventory. I must sell it—somewhere.

We package syrup principally, as do most small producers, for use in the home kitchen and sell it directly to consumers. We keep lists. Sales are prompted by mailings to customers and former customers, personal contacts where we live and work, inviting walk-ins at the saphouse during the boiling season, and keeping a shelf stocked at Hodgkins General Store in Temple village. Christmastime ads in local newspapers also bring in customers, as do word-of-mouth recommendations from our regulars to their neighbors and acquaintances. Historically, we have not experienced any difficulty selling our syrup. In fact, we're a net importer of Maine syrup since going into the business in 1964, buying wholesale or bulk syrup from local producers, blending it with a bit of our own, grading it and packaging it in our own containers.

Unlike many of our competitors, however, we have been able to avoid wholesale marketing. We've never felt a need to sell syrup at less than the retail price. We're a small producer meeting the needs of the table-top market within our sphere of visibility. Though we will frequently buy a quantity of syrup to meet our year-round retail demand, selling purchased syrup in the wholesale market forsakes the margin that comes with retail sales, and leaves little or no room for profit. So we have shied away from a wholesale price structure, and limited our selling to retail sales—except for Maggie's General Store in Freeport.

Maggie's General Store is a Freeport institution. Located on busy U.S. Route 1, which virtually 90 percent of Maine's northbound tourists use to reach interior Maine, Maggie's is the last watering hole and gasoline stop before the de rigueur visit to L.L. Bean, world renowned Freeport, Maine, outdoor icon and sporting goods outfitter. Maggie's savvy proprietor, Elaine Polakewich, a bustling Freeport businesswoman and operant, tries to stop as many of them as she can. She advertises and sells motorist services: gasoline, hot coffee, cold beverages, and newspapers. Sightseers can also pick up a complimentary copy of Maine's Official Highway Map at Maggie's.

Polakewich in the 1960s also owned and operated Maggie's Mountain, a small ski area just down Desert Road behind her general store comprising a five-hundred-foot rope tow and a small lodge that catered to skiers unfamiliar with the snowbound mountains in western Maine. Her ski area lasted until about 1970 when she gave up on her pretty much snowless Maine coast skiing adventure, and put her energy into the general store. Maggie, as she's known around Freeport, does not bypass opportunity.

Maggie calls me one day. "Can I buy pure Maine syrup from you wholesale?" she queries. "I want pure Maine syrup for the tourists who stop here for gas and a map, and the campers and the fishermen who need the real deal on their pancakes, pure Maine maple syrup." Maggie wants to put it on her shelves and advertise it on the sign out front. She emphasizes it has to be Maine-labeled pure maple syrup.

Maggie piques my interest, and we talk more. She knows, as I do, that Maine-produced pure maple syrup cannot be purchased from L.L. Bean. L.L. Bean sells Vermont-produced and Vermont-labeled pure maple syrup in its Freeport retail store and catalog. Maggie sees an opportunity. She wants to stop more of the traffic headed for the L.L. Bean retail store and thinks Maine maple syrup will do it. "I'll give 'em a choice," she says.

"Maybe the Maine maple syrup will bring 'em into my place—and they'll pick up a hot dog and a cup of coffee, too. Maybe some pancake mix."

I can't resist her. I don't want to. I'll find the syrup for Maggie. "Yes," I answer. I take her some, and she puts up a sign out front that boasts, "Get pure Maine maple syrup and the *New York Times* here!"

Maggie calls me often, and I take her a carload of pints and quarts. She compliments me often, too. And I'm careful to treat her right. "Folks love your maple syrup," she tells me more than once.

"Must be 'cause it's fresh," I answer.

My success at Maggie's, and Maggie's success at her general store, prompts me to pursue additional wholesale customers. I decide to broaden the mix, move away from exclusively pancake customers toward an even wider wholesale market. With increased production on Orchard Hill Road coming from plastic tubing and applied vacuum, the need for more market is evident. I'm producing too much syrup for the current retail customer base. Notwithstanding Brud's advice from Poughkeepsie that we need more retail customers, I look for a wider wholesale market. As it will turn out, I find it—and much more.

I have long been intrigued by L.L. Bean as a potential outlet for our maple syrup. The world-renowned sporting goods and outfitting store in Freeport, who stops, it's said, 90 percent of the sporting traffic coming into Maine, much of it in the middle of the night bound upstate to fish, hunt, and camp in the northern Maine woods, sells only pure Vermont-produced maple syrup. I don't know the quantity of syrup L.L. Bean sells, but I do know, as do Maine producers Bob Smith, Ray Titcomb, and others who have raised the subject of Maine syrup with L.L. Bean, that Maine-produced and Maine-labeled maple syrup is not sold at the L.L. Bean retail store, not even as a demonstration or an experiment.

The MMPA Board of Directors knows, too, of L.L. Bean's recalcitrance and often discusses possible ways to persuade L.L. Bean to stock Maine syrup. But to no avail. Smith has been repulsed. Letters from Titcomb and others have gone unanswered. L.L. Bean in 1982 is absent pure Maine maple syrup on its shelves.

L.L. Bean is good for Maine, has been for eighty-five years since it started selling outdoor gear. L.L. Bean promotes Maine fishing and hunting, uses Maine craftsmen in its factories, sells Maine-made products in its catalog and retail store. L.L. Bean employs Maine residents, and contributes liberally to Maine charities, offers discounts to schools and scout troops, and purchases services—printing, maintenance, cleaning—from Maine firms. L.L. Bean promotes use of Maine's outdoor recreational facilities, and its employees—volunteer crews—engage in improving Maine's hiking trails and campsites. L.L. Bean is a good neighbor, as well as good for the Maine economy. The lack of Maine maple syrup, however, in its store or in its catalog seems to me an anomaly. L.L. Bean, and its exclusive stocking of Vermont-produced maple syrup, is not following its own script.

Leon Gorman, grandson of Leon Leonwood Bean and president and chief executive officer of L.L. Bean, lives in Yarmouth, and serves on the Boy Scout Troop 35 Troop Committee. I am chair of the committee. Gorman and I are acquaintances. Following a meeting one evening in 1982, we talk maple syrup. "You don't stock Maine syrup in the store," I say to Gorman. "I'd like to see Maine syrup there. How about trying a sample of my syrup? Put it on the shelf beside the Vermont syrup. See what happens."

Gorman, a thoughtful man of relatively few words, asks me a question or two about my involvement in maple syrup production, my capacity to supply what he might need, and whether I can furnish evidence of product liability insurance. Then he writes a name and a telephone number on a piece of paper. "Here, take this," he says. "Call Deb, she'll help you."

I let a couple of days go by and then call Deb, an L.L. Bean buyer. "We'll take eight cases of twelve quarts each," she answers. "Deliver them to the West Street warehouse with an invoice."

Three weeks later, Deb calls me. "Your syrup sells great," she exclaims. "Bring us another eight cases."

We're in. I think. We no longer have to wrestle or fret over whether we can sell all we can make. Deb has heard me when I promise her I will have Maine syrup whenever she calls. Now, it's me that's holding the well-known tiger by the tail.

Deb calls often. I'm delighted. L.L. Bean purchases Maine-labeled syrup from us in quart sizes—just the right amount for a weekend camping or fishing trip to upstate Maine—and in exceptional quantities. The phone at the Hodgkins General Store in Temple, where Bill sits behind the counter now, rings—and rings. During the week leading up to Christmas 1982, Deb calls twice, the second time for us to replace a Vermont syrup order delayed in delivery. Occasionally, Jackson Mountain Farm scrambles to deliver L.L. Bean syrup promptly. But I keep my promise to Gorman. Syrup is available for L.L. Bean whenever Deb calls. In 1982 Jackson Mountain Farm sells 540 gallons of maple syrup, supplementing our own production with purchases of bulk Maine maple syrup that we grade and package under our own label. Such packaging of bulk syrup is common practice in Maine, and it is necessary at Jackson Mountain Farm for us to keep the promise to L.L.Bean. Syrup, of course, is plentiful in Maine during the latter part of 1982, many producers having, as we did at Jackson Mountain Farm, suffered exemplary production.

Jackson Mountain Farm purchases syrup from two Maine producers, both local: Ray Titcomb in Farmington, and Hartley Farmer in Temple. Titcomb, a direct descendent of Stephen Titcomb, who first made syrup in the District of Maine in 1781, operates Maine Maple Products, Inc., on Titcomb Hill in Farmington. In 1950 Titcomb sugared and managed a dairy on Titcomb Hill—Titcomb Hill Farm—and produced two hundred gallons of pure Maine maple syrup annually and 150 quarts of raw milk daily for home delivery. Ten years following the purchase of Titcomb Hill Farm, Titcomb, an industrious entrepreneur who also has owned a Farmington restaurant and served on the Board of Trustees of a Farmington bank, had grown his dairy business to five thousand quarts of pasteurized and homogenized milk daily. His delivery route included every town in Franklin County. Satisfied with his achievement, but likely also somewhat weary—he sold Titcomb Hill Farm in 1971, built a log cabin on Chain of Ponds in Eustis, Maine, and worked as a Maine guide for the next ten years.

In 1981, following his ten years recreating in the outdoors, ten years which also included whitewater canoe racing on Maine rivers with paddling partner Brud Hodgkins, Titcomb reacquired Titcomb Hill Farm, purchased the Orlando Small sugar maple acreage in Industry, Maine, and formed Maine Maple Products, Inc. When he needed to buy syrup to meet the demand, he went to northern Somerset County and the Maine Maple Sugar District, a consortium of Canadian sugarmakers operating in Maine, and purchased bulk syrup, processed and regraded it, and packaged it under his own label.

We also buy syrup from Farmer's Maple Syrup. Hartley Farmer grew up in Temple. A Vietnam War veteran, he came home and started a construction business building concrete foundations for new housing in southern Franklin County. Restless, he branched into renovation carpentry and buying and selling old houses. Farmer is a cofounder—with Dick Blodgett, local carpenter and also a descendent of early settlers—of the Temple Historical Society. His roots in Temple go back to 1807, and he has often been overheard saying he'd like to "spend thirty days back there sometime and see what it was really like." In the early 1980s he returned to his culture. He bought six milking cows and built a small barn to house them.

In 1981 Farmer sees the boom coming in maple syrup production and moves into sugaring to supplement his dairy farming. He thins a piece of woodland near his home—on Varnum Pond Road, about a mile from Orchard Hill—into a grove of sugar maples, builds a saphouse, and puts in a thousand tapholes connected to a tubing network, all in time for the 1982 sap run. I help him. And he turns to me for advice from time to time, as well. I know that if things go well for him I'll need his syrup.

Farmer makes excellent maple syrup, so good that I easily mistake the taste of it for my own. Given our deal with L.L. Bean, I offer to purchase his entire crop—estimated to be as much as 125 gallons—and furnish him empty Jackson Mountain Farm one-quart containers to package it in. He accepts the offer on condition that he set aside a portion of his production for family and friends, and a bit more to sell from his home. I agree. With Titcomb and Farmer both in, I feel we have sufficient syrup resource to meet the demand at L.L. Bean, as well as our usual cadre of retail customers, without resorting to bulk purchases.

Bulk syrup is actually available to us. Opportunity to buy fifty-gallon drums of syrup from Somerset County, or from Vermont and New York, exist for us, as well as for Titcomb and other packers. But we rarely do so. It's important for me to know and observe the practices of a producer. Tracking the pathway of bulk syrup from some distant origin to our place is beyond the realm of my daily routine. I want high-class syrup. Titcomb and Farmer, local producers we can observe and trust, deliver it.

Our relationship with L.L. Bean continues into the mid-1980s. The experiment I offered Leon Gorman works out well. Pure Maine-labeled maple syrup in the L.L. Bean retail store side by side with Vermont-labeled syrup has proved so successful that Maine producer Bob Smith of Skowhegan is also able to persuade Bean to display Maine syrup for sale, syrup packaged in half-pint cans shaped to resemble a sugar shack. I suspect that Maine syrup now outsells the Vermont brand in the retail store.

In late 1983 Brud and I decide to pitch the L.L. Bean catalog. "We have the syrup," I appeal to Brud. "What we don't have is clout, someone that can convince Bean that we have the ability to deliver."

"I'll bring Ray Titcomb with me," Brud answers, "and the marketing chief at the Department of Agriculture. You ask for Leon. Call Deb and set it up."

I know from my discussion with Gorman that I will need a convincing argument. He will need to know that we control sufficient syrup, and I, for one, don't know whether we do or not. Or whether Ray Titcomb does. But I do know that Maine syrup in the retail store is outselling L.L. Bean's projections. And that our service is faultless. And I know that Ray Titcomb controls a plentiful amount of syrup in Somerset County. Perhaps that will be enough. Perhaps we won't need to produce financial security, simply a guarantee of performance.

But we don't know enough about the amount of syrup L.L. Bean sells via the catalog. I know it is considerable, perhaps even a hundred thousand gallons yearly, so we plan to take Ray Titcomb with us. Titcomb's maple syrup sources may be inexhaustible. Producers in Somerset County are expanding rapidly, and Titcomb, who furnishes valuable assistance to the producers up there, holds insider status with all of them and currently purchases as much as seventy-five thousand gallons to meet his annual need. Titcomb, I sense, will be the key person in our presentation. I call Deb and ask her to arrange a meeting.

We meet in September at the L.L. Bean retail store in Freeport. Stuart McGeorge, L.L. Bean product manager, is there. Jackson Mountain Farm's three partners, Brud, Bill, and I, come. Ray Titcomb, whose Maine Maple Products, Inc. will be our supplier, is there. Leon Gorman is not there, nor is anyone from the Maine Department of Agriculture. It's McGeorge and us.

McGeorge acknowledges our proposal and concedes that our syrup has sold well in the retail store, tastes fine, and that he is proud to be selling Maine syrup. But he turns down our request for a listing in the catalog—and, in my opinion, for a very good reason. L.L. Bean will remain loyal to their long-time Vermont vendor who has served them well for many years. "I appreciate your continued interest in L.L. Bean," McGeorge tells us, "and L.L. Bean is pleased to continue to offer your Maine syrup for sale in our retail store."

I go away peacefully, satisfied that I have been able to fashion a sit-down meeting with high-level L.L. Bean management, and relieved that McGeorge has endorsed our syrup and its continued supply to the retail store which, of course, will likely spread to other Maine producers as well. And he keeps his promise to us. Deliveries to the West Street warehouse go on for several more years. Then in 1988, the phone stops ringing. It's been a good run, I think. But it may be over.

After a time, perhaps a few months, I call Deb. "Thank you for allowing us to be the first Maine producer to sell pure Maine maple syrup in your store," I say. "It's been a good run for us." She mentions something about changes in the store, and I respond by giving her Ray Titcomb's telephone number. "If you need some syrup, buy it from Ray," I tell her. "He'll treat you right."

Soon I notice L.L. Bean–labeled pure maple syrup in the retail store, and in the catalog as well. The label identifies it as packaged in Maine and Vermont. But the label doesn't tell me where the syrup actually comes from; just that it is packaged in Maine and Vermont. Word in the saphouses is that a Vermont syrup packer has purchased Titcomb's Maine Maple Products and packages syrup from Somerset County and from drum producers in Vermont for the L.L. Bean account. Obviously, L.L. Bean has discovered value in Maine-produced pure maple syrup.

The loss of L.L. Bean as a customer does not leave me with nothing to do. I am an agent for the Leader Evaporator Company in Maine, president of the Maine Maple Producers Association, and I'm alone at Jackson Mountain Farm. Brud and Bill have withdrawn from active participation. Maine sugaring is changing, and I need to catch up. I focus my attention on Jackson Mountain Farm and its loyal table-top customers, one gallon at a time.

CHAPTER SIXTEEN

THE MAINE MAPLE
PRODUCERS ASSOCIATION

AT THE MAINE MAPLE PRODUCERS ASSOCIATION'S ANNUAL MEETING at the Augusta Civic Center in January 1983, the membership elects me to the MMPA Board of Directors. I have been an MMPA member since 1965 when Brud and I attended the annual meeting and maple trade show held then in the Lewiston Armory concurrent with the annual Lewiston Agricultural Trade Show. Election to the board is a first for me and a first for anyone representing Jackson Mountain Farm.

The board comprises the president of MMPA, the vice president, secretary-treasurer, and six at-large directors. Two at-large directors are elected to three-year terms each year. Linwood Foster of Skowhegan, also a first-timer in 1983, is elected to the board with me. The other four directors, elected to staggered terms, are working off their time, so to speak. My three-year term—and Foster's—starts following this meeting. I don't know where to begin. I find a copy of the bylaws and look for what directors are expected to do. I discover that the board, according to Article V, performs "those duties usually pertaining to such offices."

The 1983 board holds its first meeting a month later, February 8, in Skowhegan. I am attentive to the agenda. President Arnold Luce introduces the subject of marketing and proposes an annual celebration, a saphouse open house with tours, education, and eats, to promote and sell pure Maine maple syrup. Questions follow Luce's proposal, such as "When will it be held?" and "Who will come?" Discussion occurs. Finally, right there in Jack Steeves's parlor, the board votes unanimously to create a Maine Maple Sunday™. Just like that. A day, or perhaps a weekend, set aside for Maine sugarmakers to host open houses and celebrate Maine sugarmaking. We set the date of the first celebration for March 27, 1983, the fourth Sunday in March, barely six weeks away. "What will we call it?" someone asks. I respond, "How about Maine Maple Sunday?" And then, following more discussion and a bit of other miscellaneous agenda, the meeting is over. I didn't know it then, but that meeting will become the most memorable board meeting in MMPA history.

The Maine Maple Producers Association, which in 1983 numbered perhaps a hundred licensed Maine producers, dates to 1945 when pieces of several county-based producer groups in Oxford, Franklin, Somerset, and Penobscot counties met in Augusta at the University of Maine's Cooperative Extension Service office in December to discuss the formation of a statewide organization. Kenneth Cooper, Buckfield maple producer and head of the Oxford County group, requested the meeting. A. D. Nutting, Extension Service forestry specialist, organized it. Out of Cooper's idea, the Maine Maple Producers Association came into being at that meeting, bylaws and all.

The new MMPA held its first statewide meeting in March 1946 at the Maine State Grange Headquarters in Augusta. Thirty-six producers—the charter members—elected Richard Eaton of East Corinth president, Orlando Small of Farmington vice president, and Kenneth Cooper of Buckfield secretary. These officers and Leon Witham, Oakland, and Arthur Johnston, Washington, at-large delegates, made up the first board of directors.

The charter members then agreed that the primary mission of the association would be promotion of maple syrup and its subsequent products and MMPA representation in regulatory matters at the Maine statehouse. Its work also, in addition to promotion and regulatory matters, would include providing information, education, and training to producers. The member producers present adopted the bylaws unanimously and fixed the membership dues at $1 per year.

The first bylaws, which tracked similar bylaws used in adjoining New Hampshire, set forth the objectives of the fledgling association: first, promote and publicize pure Maine maple syrup, its subsequent products, and the interests of maple syrup producers in Maine; second, promote education and exchange ideas of mutual interest with Maine producers; third, promote and support increased development of the maple industry in Maine; and fourth, promote proper grading and standardization of maple products. The association also bound itself in its bylaws to cooperate with the Maine Experiment Station, the Cooperative Extension Service, and the State Department of Agriculture in developing a progressive program for the maple industry in Maine.

The 1946 business meeting centered on maple syrup prices. Grade A or Fancy syrup sold then for something less than $5 per gallon in gallon containers and somewhat more per gallon in pint- and quart-sized containers, prices that likely came from polling the producers at the meeting, though Secretary Cooper did not record any action by the board.

By 1947 MMPA membership had risen to 125 producers. At the annual meeting, Secretary Cooper reported that the association, as required by its bylaws, had established a registered label for use by its members on Maine maple syrup packaged for sale. The label featured a blue, white, and red trademark symbol and was approved for Maine-produced agricultural products by the Department of Agriculture. Producers would be assessed a $1 fee for permission to affix the label to their maple products.

In 1948, promotional activity began to show up at MMPA. Promoting syrup sales at Maine agricultural fairs came first. Maine producers brought pure Maine maple syrup to Bangor, Skowhegan, Farmington, and Oxford fairs and displayed it in the exhibition halls and fair booths. At the close of the fair season, MMPA donated samples of Maine-branded syrup to the governor, the legislature, and other government notables together with such promotional material as photographs and publicity for their use in promoting Maine products in their hometowns. Later in 1948, Buckfield producer Cooper, then vice president of MMPA, and John Wilder of Norridgewock each hosted fertilizer demonstrations in their maple orchards for MMPA members in cooperation with the

University of Maine Cooperative Extension Service and several fertilizer dealers. And at the MMPA annual meeting the following January, equipment dealers featured an exhibit and demonstration of the innovative gasoline-powered tapping machine, all the result of MMPA's proactive promotion of Maine maple syrup.

During the years following 1948, local meetings continued to be held in the various counties, followed by the annual statewide meeting just in advance of the sugaring season. The county meetings faded somewhat, however, as time passed, and by 1965 when the MMPA annual meeting first appeared in the Lewiston Armory, MMPA county meetings had disappeared. The membership continued to meet at an annual meeting in January of each year.

In 1967 Brud and I attend the annual meeting again, this time also at the Lewiston Armory. A sample of our best-tasting syrup is entered in the state contest, and we're anxious to learn the outcome. The room is full again, and we migrate to the back, maybe twenty rows back from the head table where the officers and directors sit. When the time comes, the president distributes the contest results to the crowd. Entrants in the contest also receive an additional single sheet breaking their score into its elements: color, density, clarity, and taste. Jackson Mountain Farm places twelfth—out of twelve entries. I'm mortified. But not one to call attention to myself, I sit motionless and remain quiet so as not to be recognized as the producer of the twelfth-place syrup. My syrup is the worst here, I moan, and I feel everyone's eyes on me. My analysis of the judges' evaluation, however, leads me to conclude that I'm getting more value from a low score than I would as a winner, since a winner has only a lonesome ribbon to take home. I'm learning what I do wrong, what I don't get right. In this case, it's what the judges call a cloud in my syrup. I relax. I can fix that—I think.

The discussion at the head table turns to the Yarmouth Clam Festival, an annual three-day summer gala in my hometown attended by some say fifty thousand people. The festival's committee, the speaker says, desires somehow to market Maine maple syrup at the festival. I am compelled to stand and talk. "I was contacted by the festival last July," I say. "It's a promotion of Maine clams and lobsters, not maple syrup. But to be cooperative, I took the committee a hundred gallons or so in consumer-sized containers and when the festival ended, they returned it all. They don't know what to do with maple syrup." My comments end the discussion of the Yarmouth Clam Festival. I escape the meeting unharmed and bound to remove the cloud from my maple syrup.

In 1967, the MMPA's portable saphouse—mounted on a flat-bed trailer that can be towed here and there—makes its debut at the Sugarloaf Mountain Ski Area in Carrabassett Valley. An instant hit, it prompts many questions and offers the association opportunity to publicize the Maine maple industry beyond Maine's borders. The saphouse on wheels also appears at the Strong Maple Festival in April. Its popularity eventually leads to the construction of stationary saphouses at five Maine agricultural fairs: Fryeburg, Farmington, Cumberland, Skowhegan, and the Common Ground fair in Windsor.

The Maine Maple Producers Association does not meet again in Lewiston. In 1973 a Maine Agricultural Trade Show appears in the new Augusta Civic Center, and MMPA follows. The annual trade showpiece is improved some by then, and features separate promotion booths on the exhibit floor for associations and agricultural vendors. Meeting rooms—small auditoriums, actually—throughout the Civic Center are available for workshop sessions and annual meetings. MMPA erects a promotional booth on the exhibit floor and brings its annual meeting to the Civic Center as well. Several maple supply vendors—Leader Evaporator Company is the first—follow the association to Augusta.

The Maine Agricultural Trade Show continues to be a January feature at the Augusta Civic Center. Each year in January, the MMPA rents discounted space on the exhibit floor, fills the rented space with promotional materials—brochures, posters, photos, maple syrup displays, membership sign-up sheets, and perhaps a rolling slideshow—and engages passersby in maple talk, carrying out MMPA's mission to promote maple syrup and its subsequent products.

In February 1983, MMPA, to improve its promotional portfolio, publishes its first newsletter, *Maine Maple Newsletter*. Ted Greene, East Sebago maple producer and secretary of the association, compiles and writes the first issue, which features topics centered on the promotion and marketing of Maine-made maple syrup. "Several ideas and suggestions have been made," Greene writes, "to promote pure Maine maple syrup. This newsletter is one." Though intended to be a quarterly publication, MMPA distributes its newsletter to members perhaps twice each year, once before the annual meeting and again in the early summer following the sap run. In 2001, however, largely at the insistence of members who continue to question the value they receive for their $15 membership dues, the association settles on a quarterly publication, changes the newsletter's name to *Maple News*, and increases its content. By 2015 it is a ten-page document full of news, photographs, advertisements, and editorial comment. Membership dues are $55 annually.

In 1989, following two terms as director, I am elected vice president of the MMPA and placed in the hierarchical pipeline leading to the presidency. I am honored. I am also aware that my service on the board to date has not been exemplary, though I did play a role in the creation of Maine Maple Sunday and paid my dues, so to speak, on various committees. In turn, I have also staffed maple promotion booths here and there, most notably the Maine Mall in South Portland and the Augusta Civic Center, and otherwise helped to move Maine's sugaring industry forward.

Early in my vice presidency the MMPA hosts the annual fall meeting of the combined North American Maple Syrup Council and International Maple Syrup Institute, the two most significant—and powerful—maple associations in the maple world. It is our first attempt at hosting such a prestigious and noteworthy meeting, and I am chair of the organizing committee. We invite maple officials from every maple-producing state and province, including their spouses and guests. In addition to maple officials, the meeting brings together maple producers, maple processors, maple equipment manufacturers, and maple researchers. We expect three hundred people. We finance the start-up costs with annual dues—the board enacted a $10 increase in 1987—and establish a registration fee to cover all remaining costs.

The convention is held in South Portland near the ocean, in a high-rise Hilton hotel, a four-day weekend in October. Sunny and warm. Ted (T. A.) Greene, dressed in a checkered shirt, denim jeans, sporting a gray beard, and showing off a Maine twang—"We grow 'taters up here, too. An' cut our own coddwood"—is the keynote speaker, a slide show of Maine sugaring. During the four days, MMPA puts on a gala affair that includes an agenda of presentations on the techniques of producing maple syrup, an exhibit—trade show—of vendors displaying the latest in maple supplies and equipment, a maple syrup contest, business meetings, committee meetings, and off-site tours of iconic Maine. Our three hundred guests tour western Maine saphouses, take a boat ride on Casco Bay, shop at L.L. Bean in Freeport, and feast at an authentic lobster bake offshore on House Island in Casco Bay. At the final banquet, I am the featured speaker and spend twenty minutes praising the virtues of pure Maine maple syrup—"tastes so good we can sell it in a paper bag." It's a bountiful four days of celebrating sugaring in Maine, all hosted by the Maine Maple Producers Association, which enjoys a very profitable weekend.

Later on, January 2003, the MMPA Board approves the formation of geographical subchapters bound to the objectives of the association and the MMPA bylaws and rules. The Somerset County Sugarmakers Association is first; the Southern Maine Maple Sugarmakers Association is second. The spread of subchapters into the countryside, so to speak, emphasizes the value of MMPA. It brings sugarmakers together from every corner of Maine.

Chapter Seventeen

THE MAINE MAPLE SUGAR DISTRICT

In 1935, in the midst of the Great Depression, 197 sugar shacks dotted the landscape along Maine's northwestern border with Canada. The sugar shacks reached from Dole Pond north of Jackman northerly to Harwood Mountain, using up a total area of nine Maine townships over some five hundred square miles—320,000 acres—of Maine hardwood forest in Somerset County.

Two paper companies, Great Northern Paper and International Paper, owned the forest then. Sugar maples were plentiful along the border, and each spring since before the turn of the twentieth century Quebeckers from the nearby saint-named towns of Saint-Côme, Saint-Zacharie, Saint-Aurélie, Saint-Louis, Saint-Cyprien, and Saint-Justin who didn't have ownership or access to equivalent land on their own side of the border crossed into Maine and, for a per-taphole fee paid to the paper tycoons, set up sugar shacks and tapped sugar maple trees.

At each saphouse they hung buckets, perhaps as many as three thousand, gathered the sap on snowshoes, and conveyed it to their sugar shack in wooden tubs mounted on horse-drawn sledges. There, they boiled off the sap into a table-grade topping French Canadians called *sirop d'érable*, packed it in kegs and casks—later in fifty-gallon steel drums—and transported it back across the border to Quebec. In Quebec, they sold the *sirop* to Vermonters and New Yorkers, where packers reprocessed, graded, and packaged it for the retail maple syrup market.

In the beginning, long before 1935, say about 1880, the Quebeckers boiled their sap in cast iron cauldrons, sometimes three over a fire at once, and produced seven or so drums of syrup each year per saphouse. They made grade C syrup mostly, sometimes grade D, very dark. They couldn't make light syrup in the cauldrons or even in the early flat-pan evaporators, nor did they want to. The Quebeckers boiled their sap deep and slow and made their syrup dark and strong, as they preferred it.

By the 1970s the number of Quebec sugar camps in what was then called the Maine Maple Sugar District had fallen to seventy. Each family tended perhaps as many as six thousand buckets. At least one, Jean Bisson, who sugared on International Paper land, sugared the old-fashioned way, firing an outsized open-pan evaporator with split hardwood logs—likely split in the summer by Jean himself—taken from International Paper lands. Aime, another Bisson, drew off syrup for Jean. The family worked on snowshoes gathering sap by hand and sledge.

The Bissons produced eight hundred imperial gallons of maple syrup in 1973, according to Maine Bureau of Forestry's maple syrup specialist Walter Gooley, 2 percent of the forty thousand gallons produced in the Maine Maple Sugar District that year, a year when the production in the district fell 20 percent short of its customary fifty thousand gallons. Bisson—and other Sugar District producers as well—shipped their syrup in fifty-gallon steel drums to Sherbrooke, Quebec, where it was auctioned, primarily to buyers from Vermont. Ironically, the U.S. Department of Agriculture reported in 1973 that licensed Maine producers produced eight thousand U.S. gallons of syrup statewide, a mere 20 percent of the pure maple syrup produced in the sugar district alone by the unlicensed Canadians.

Change came to the sugar district in 1981. Maine sugarmaker Raymond Titcomb, back from a ten-year sugaring hiatus fly fishing out the back door of a log cabin in Eustis, reacquired the Titcomb Hill Dairy Farm, added the Orlando Small sugarbush in nearby Industry to his sugar maple resources, and formed Maine Maple Products, Inc. Titcomb, an experienced and aggressive businessman, yet also an advocate of a fair deal and satisfied customers, added maple syrup to his delivery-route products and expanded his market to virtually all retail and wholesale milk and syrup buyers in Franklin and Somerset counties. Sales, especially of maple syrup, grew rapidly. Soon he was outselling his production and was in urgent need of a supplier of bulk syrup. He turned to the Canadian producers in the Maine Maple Sugar District.

The Quebeckers then were packing their Maine production in fifty-gallon steel drums and shipping it to retail and wholesale packers in Vermont and New York. From there, the syrup made its way to retail shelves and consumers outside both Maine and Quebec. Titcomb saw opportunity in the Maine Maple Sugar District. He traveled there and acquired syrup for himself, reprocessed it, graded it, packed it in consumer-sized containers as Maine maple syrup, and then distributed it to his customers throughout Maine. Though the syrup was actually made in Maine, it was made by unlicensed producers, and Titcomb's competitors felt it should not be labeled as pure Maine maple syrup. Competing producers in Maine, some of whom wholesaled syrup to the same retailers, complained publicly that Titcomb was not actually packing Maine maple syrup in his containers as the label indicated and as the Maine grading law required. A small flap ensued, and the Maine Attorney General's office was drawn into the fracas, as were the Maine Department of Agriculture and other Maine producers.

The Department of Agriculture found evidence of labeling violations, and not just on Titcomb Hill. Several large Maine producers and packers admitted packaging bulk syrup purchased in the sugar district, as well as in other states, and selling it as Maine made. The packers argued that as long as the syrup was reprocessed, graded, and packaged in consumer-sized containers in Maine, the law allowed it to be labeled Maine made. Maine's Attorney General disagreed, describing the practice as a violation of Maine's truth-in-labeling law.

The Department of Agriculture soon recognized a need to clarify its labeling regulations and bring a conclusion to the labeling dither. In 1983, the department published new regulations. All syrup labeled as pure Maine maple syrup must be produced—meaning made—in the state of Maine. The department also established a state licensing requirement that obliged a producer to be licensed—at a fee payable to the state—to produce and sell maple syrup in Maine. These regulations effectively put the sugar district—the Quebeckers in northern Somerset County—out of the business they were in. Titcomb, who freely admitted that he had graded, packed, and sold the disputed syrup, and who was reportedly buying 90 percent of the Maine Maple Sugar District production, reacted quickly.

Titcomb rushed to bring the sugar district's drum suppliers into compliance with Maine law. He furnished the Quebeckers with Maine regulations and equipped them with hydrometers, grading kits, and effective syrup filters. He assisted them in the Maine licensing process and watched over their sugarmaking for the next year or so, as did the Maine Department of Agriculture. And he assured the Department of Agriculture that sugar district producers were properly qualified and licensed to produce Maine syrup for sale in Maine. By 1985 the Quebeckers were properly equipped and certified to produce Maine maple syrup suitable for the Maine market and in accordance with Maine regulations. This action by Titcomb enabled the expansion and sale of authentic Maine-labeled syrup produced in northern Somerset County such that Titcomb could acquire high-quality Maine maple syrup without delay whenever he needed it. In 1988 the U.S. Department of Agriculture included syrup produced in the sugar district in the official Maine production count. Maine reported seventy-six thousand gallons of maple syrup produced that year, up from five thousand gallons the year before.

Titcomb continued to manage Maine Maple Products, Inc. throughout the 1980s and early 1990s. Maine's syrup production during this period reached a reported 150,000 gallons, the greater part of it produced in the Maine Maple Sugar District by Quebeckers and sold to Maine packers—including Titcomb. In 1994, the time came for Titcomb to retire again. He sold Maine Maple Products, Inc. to Marc and Hélène Larivière of Saint-Zacharie, Quebec, and left for Florida, after a long and distinguished career in Maine sugaring.

The Larivières relocated Maine Maple Products, Inc. from Titcomb Hill in Farmington to Madison, Maine, and continued to package and wholesale syrup on Titcomb's distribution routes. The Larivières' syrup resource then comprised what they produced in Somerset County and what two other neighboring producers in the sugar district could come up with, a total of about 145,000 tapholes or a bit more than thirty thousand gallons of syrup yearly. Eric Ellis, who started sugaring for Ray Titcomb in 1978 at age twelve and now manages Maine Maple Products, Inc. for the Larivières in Madison, credits the Larivières' success to the use of new sugaring technology and the distribution routes first established by Raymond Titcomb, the same Raymond Titcomb who discovered the potential value of the Maine Maple Sugar District to Maine producers and packers; the same Raymond Titcomb who first brought *sirop d'érable* to Maine's syrup customers as certified Maine maple syrup; and the same Raymond Titcomb who launched Maine's climb in the syrup production count that would eventually bring Maine into the top two of the fourteen maple syrup–producing states. When Raymond Titcomb, the last of the Stephen Titcomb descendants to make syrup on Titcomb Hill in Farmington, left sugaring in 1994, Maine produced thirty times as much maple syrup annually—150,000 gallons—as it did in 1980 when he went into the sugaring business. In 2014, ten years later, Michael Bryant, secretary of MMPA, reported forty-five saphouses and more than one million tapholes producing more than 300,000 gallons of maple syrup in the Maine Maple Sugar District each year.

Titcomb's legacy, however, centers on the syrup he produced on Titcomb Hill. It was not a complicated business for him. He was a student of the art, so to speak, the go-to person for sugarmakers such as Brud and me. Light syrup was highly desirable then, admired as much for its appearance atop a pancake as for its taste. Titcomb kept his syrup-making processes organized and clean, boiled sap shallow and quick, and produced some of the lightest syrup in the county. He was one of the first to conserve fuel; during the energy crises in the 1970s and 1980s, he squirted a bit of waste motor oil into his firebox frequently to stabilize his fire and to conserve his woodpile. Titcomb was stoic and assured in his ways, a legitimate heir to his ancestor Stephen's pioneer toughness. Titcomb was as good as I've seen. When Jackson Mountain Farm needs to purchase maple syrup, we call Ray Titcomb first.

Sometime in the 1990s Al Bolduc and Bob Smith, MMPA members who also sugared in Somerset County, organized the sugar district producers into the Somerset County Sugarmakers Association and requested status from MMPA. After some discussion and the passage of considerable time, the MMPA board approved the request. Currently, producers in the Somerset County Sugarmakers Association produce more than 90 percent of the maple syrup made in Maine.

Chapter Eighteen

CHANGE COMES TO ORCHARD HILL

It's 1990. Brud is gone, has been for several years except for an occasional visit now and then. Gone, too, is Bill, gone to tend the general store and his family, though when I'm desperate for someone to lift the other end of something heavy or bulky he comes to the saphouse and helps me. Jackson Mountain Farm is just a ten-acre lot now, comprising second-growth sugar maples—a dite less than six hundred tapholes—in a thirty-acre portion of the Temple Oaks Subdivision. And it's ours, Beth and me. We will sugar as many of the six hundred as we think we can manage alone.

First, we slim down. Our existing boiling process is old and heavy, cumbersome and inefficient, just too much to face on a February morning of a new sugaring season. We discard the five-by-fourteen Leader Special. Though it still sits in the saphouse and produces six gallons of beautiful Maine maple syrup every hour, I don't need it. It's too big. We purchased the big rig in 1964, boiled with it for twenty-six years, replaced the front pan at least twice, and soldered an embarrassing number of leaks. We—Brud, Bill, and I—could handle it then. But I'm alone with Beth now, and down to six hundred tapholes. I'm buying something I can lift, keep clean, and see from one side to the other when the steam is billowing. I replace it with a rig half the size, a Leader Special three feet wide and twelve feet long. It's rated by Leader to boil off ninety-five gallons of sap per hour. I ask Bruce Gillilan, who runs the company now, to add a foot to the flue pan and shorten the front pan the same. "I'd like to get more than a hundred out of it, if I can," I tell him. I pay a bit more but I'll boil off more sap in less time, which for me translates to less fuel oil. And with the three by twelve I won't have to wrestle with heavy and bulky pans.

I build a concrete-block arch for the new pans to sit on. I start November 11, Armistice Day, and put up a plastic tent over the work area. I work in the enclosure beside a small electric heater, mortar the blocks in place in the comfort of the tent, and finish before Christmas. Frank O'Donel, my odd-jobber and advisor, comes down from Varnum Pond Road and helps me mount one of the two oil burners I salvaged from the old rig on the front of the new arch. We set the other one in a corner of the saphouse. "You'll need it for spare parts," Frank tells me. Leader delivers the new pans in January, well ahead of the first warm day in March.

The new rig, a tad less than half the hot surface of the old one, will boil off a bit more than a hundred gallons of sap an hour, more than enough evaporation for the six hundred tapholes. And the stainless steel pans, which I reason will ultimately cost less than English tin considering the damage I will avoid, will last indefinitely. Hitherto, we've gone through three scorched and wrinkled English tin front pans, and it's come to me that stainless steel will be a better deal in the long run. It's tougher, absorbs less heat, and is easily cleaned. I expect it will produce less costly syrup.

Stainless steel, also known as inox steel or inox, is remarkably heat resistant, noncorrosive, and literally stainless. But it came to sugaring slowly. Jackson Mountain Farm had the option of buying stainless steel evaporator pans—or just a stainless steel front pan—in 1964, but passed. It was not popular then, and it outclassed our meager budget, likely most other folks' budgets as well. Patented in the United States in 1919 to Elwood Haynes, inox is commonly used in kitchen sinks, cookware, bakeware, surgical tools, architecture, and such industrial equipment as valves and piping, Perhaps its most visible application is in the kitchen, but most notable is the cladding on the top portion of the Chrysler Building in

New York City. Stainless steel will align Jackson Mountain Farm with the upper tier of current Maine evaporators.

Starting on the first fair day in March 1991 and continuing for the next seven weeks, Beth and I do not lack work. We string precoded plastic tubing segments in the same locations we used last year, put in as many tapholes as we can squeeze onto the ten acres, nearly six hundred, and connect the tubing segments to lateral lines leading to the mainline. After a week we have 575 taps in, and sap is flowing into the storage tank. Nearly every day for the next four weeks, we fire the new three by twelve for an hour or two and boil off syrup. We package seventy-two gallons of maple syrup in that time, twenty-some batches, about a pint of syrup per taphole. Then time comes to take down the tubing and wash it. By mid-April, seven weeks after the first fair day in March, we're done—the perfect season, I think. We now know what the ten acres will produce.

The next year I decide to tap just half the bush. During the twelve years we've tapped Orchard Hill, I have not observed any obvious growth in tree diameter, or any sustained increase in sap yield per taphole. I wonder whether I'm asking too much of the young trees. A tree or two has actually died. Perhaps it needed an occasional rest, a year or two without being drilled. Time off to recover from its wounds. "Let's alternately rest our trees," I suggest to Beth. "Rotate the crop, so to speak. See if they'll grow faster—or sweeter."

We divide the grove. For four years we alternately tap the halves, three hundred or so tapholes. Production drops, of course. But we work less. Tapping takes less time, boiling-off is less onerous, and clean-up requires less muscle. Though I don't notice any surge in growth, I feel better about the health of my trees. Years that I don't produce enough syrup, I call Hartley Farmer on Varnum Pond Road, or Ray Titcomb on Titcomb Hill, and blend their syrup with some of my own. I don't work as hard.

By the end of the fourth season of rotating the trees, however, I feel an urge to do more, more even than the six hundred. Our market has grown. We have no chance of producing what we can sell without tapping more. And I don't see my trees responding to the time-outs, the rest periods. They're not, as best I can determine after four years, growing faster or yielding more sap. But syrup sales have grown. Demand exceeds our production. So, in 1996 we go back to drilling nearly six hundred tapholes.

The 1996 operation is state-of-the-art sugaring technology. I boast to my friends—customers, too—that I am abreast of the syrup-making technology in Maine. Though I am a small producer with less than one thousand tapholes, my tree-to-tree plastic tubing layout is the latest thinking in transporting sap. I insert vacuum—15 inHg—into the lines, which brings the sap directly to the saphouse storage tank. And I also tap and hang a dozen roadside buckets—to identify us—along Orchard Hill Road, sort of a roadside advertising sign. "Folks need to know we're making maple syrup here," I explain to a passerby.

It's been thirty-two years since I started sugaring commercially, thirty-two years since we took the pictures and created the memories on Jackson Mountain. The technology we use these days, however, bears little resemblance to the bucket and bulldozer days of 1964. It's time, I think, before the technology advances further, to record the modern method of producing maple syrup. I enlist Bill Hodgkins, my twenty-something-year-old son and a recent graduate of New England College in Henniker, New Hampshire, with a degree in communications.

Bill brings his video camera to Orchard Hill frequently during the 1996 season. "I want a video of what we do here," I tell him, "how we tap, gather, boil-off, grade, and package maple syrup. My great grandfather—your great-great grandfather—made his own maple syrup on Orchard Hill Road, perhaps in these same woods, and I want to preserve how we do it." Bill says he'll also edit the shooting and create a presentation.

Bill records more than one hundred minutes of video. It includes background music and interviews with all the participants, including siblings and spouses. He begins filming when we start putting up the tubing. "Lines are numbered and color coded," I say to the camera, "the line marked in blue-green is strung between trees marked with blue-green dots."

ALBION TRACY AT MAPLE HILL FARM IN FARMINGTON USED OXEN TO PULL A DRAY WITH A WOODEN TUB TO TRANSPORT GATHERED SAP TO THE SAPHOUSE.

THE FOUNDERS OF JACKSON MOUNTAIN MAPLE FARM: (LEFT TO RIGHT) JOHN HODGKINS, RONALD SMITH, BILL HODGKINS, BRUD HODGKINS.

SURPLUS JACKSON MOUNTAIN SYRUP WAS SOMETIMES SOLD AND DISTRIBUTED UNDER OTHER LABELS, SUCH AS THIS CIRCA 1965 FORSTER MANUFACTURING CAN.

THE SAPHOUSE ON DAY MOUNTAIN ROAD WAS AN ASSEMBLAGE OF OLD BOARDS AND TIMBERS NAILED TOGETHER BY BRUD. THE TAR PAPER FINISH WAS HELD IN PLACE BY LATHS. BOARDS EXPOSED CRACKS AND GAPS THAT LET AIR IN TO BOOST THE FIRE. WINDOWS WERE NAILED IN PLACE. THERE WASN'T A RIGHT ANGLE OR STRAIGHT LINE ANYWHERE, LIKE GRANDPA C. F. BUILT IT IN 1890. IT WAS BEAUTIFUL.

FILTERING THE SYRUP BEFORE PACKAGING, CA. 1967.

MAINE

PURE

MAPLE SYRUP

CONTENTS
ONE GALLON LIQUID
NET WT. 11 LBS.

DISTRIBUTED BY

IN 1966 WE SWITCHED FROM THE OFFICIAL MAINE DEPARTMENT OF AGRI-
CULTURE CAN TO THIS LITHOGRAPH ALL–TIN VERSION MADE BY THE STERN
CAN COMPANY OF PEABODY, MASSACHUSETTS.

THE MAINE DEPARTMENT OF AGRICULTURE CREATED THE OFFI-
CIAL BLUE, WHITE, AND RED AGRICULTURAL TRADEMARK IN THE
1930S DURING THE GREAT DEPRESSION WHEN THE NATION'S
ECONOMY WAS DORMANT AND NEEDED A BOOST. IN 1964, THE
FIRST YEAR OF MAPLE PRODUCTION AT JACKSON MOUNTAIN
MAPLE FARM, THE BLUE, WHITE, AND RED LOGO HAD BEEN
AVAILABLE FOR PERHAPS TWENTY-FIVE YEARS, AND WAS USED
BY VIRTUALLY ALL COMMERCIAL MAPLE PRODUCERS.

BRUD FEEDING THE EVAPORATOR WITH WOOD. A CORD OF WOOD PRODUCED ABOUT 25 GALLONS OF MAPLE SYRUP.

PLASTIC TUBING FOR SAP COLLECTION FIRST APPEARED IN MAINE IN 1959. WARREN VOTER, AN AGENT FOR VARIOUS MAPLE SYRUP EQUIPMENT MANUFACTURERS, DEMONSTRATED THE USE OF PLASTIC TUBING AT HIS SUGARBUSH ON VOTER HILL IN WEST FARMINGTON AND PROMOTED ITS USE.

THIS MODERN SAPHOUSE WAS BUILT IN 1978 ON ORCHARD HILL ROAD.

IN THE 1980S, PLASTIC TUBING REVOLUTIONIZED THE COLLECTION OF SAP. PRIOR TO ITS INTRODUCTION, SYRUP PRODUCERS WERE LIMITED IN THE SIZE OF THEIR OPERATION—THERE WAS ONLY SO MUCH HAULING OF SAP THEY COULD DO IN A DAY.

THE COLOR OF MAPLE SYRUP IS DETERMINED EVERY DAY—EVERY BATCH—
ACCORDING TO HOW LIGHT PASSES THROUGH IT. CONTINUAL GRADING WAS
NECESSARY BECAUSE THE SAP LOST SUGAR AS THE SEASON PROGRESSED,
DARKENING THE SYRUP SLIGHTLY AND REQUIRING MORE BOILING TO REACH
STANDARD DENSITY SYRUP.

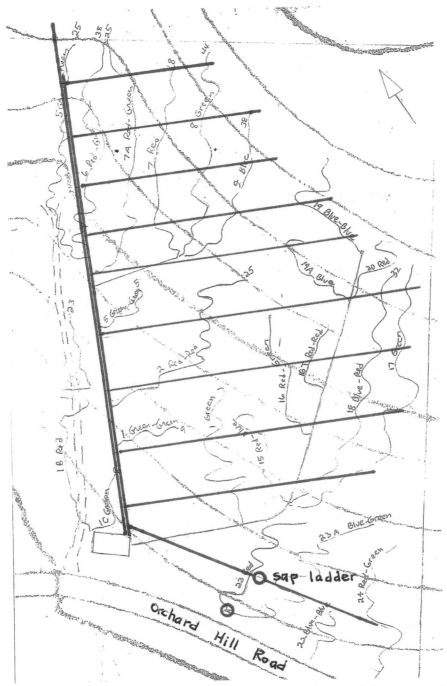

REPLACING THE TUBING LINES IN 2015 AND CHANGING TO A PROVEN AND HYDRAULICALLY EFFICIENT SYSTEM RESULTED IN A QUANTUM JUMP IN SAP YIELD—A 60 PERCENT INCREASE IN 2016.

Maine Maple Syrup Production
1965 – 2015

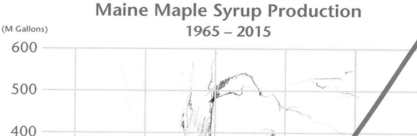

(M Gallons)

600	
500	
400	
300	
200	
100	
0	

1965 1970 1975 1980 1985 1990 1995 2000 2005 2010 2015

IN 2017, MAINE SUGARMAKERS, AFTER A REMARKABLE THIRTY-YEAR RUN IN GROWTH AND PRODUCTION OF MAPLE SYRUP, REACHED 709,000 GALLONS OF MAPLE SYRUP PRODUCED, A GROWTH PERFORMANCE RARELY ACHIEVED FOR ANY MANUFACTURED OR AGRICULTURAL PRODUCT.

Bill also films expository that I provide at critical points along the way. "The final test for quality is to taste it," I say as I sip a bit out of a sample cup. "If it doesn't taste good, it's not good." He cues the interviews, as well. "Do you have a favorite story?" he queries his siblings, "maybe a ride in the back of the old red Chevy?"

The filming features the family, all seven of us somehow engaged in the process of sugaring from setting taps to washing the floor at the end of the season. Bill interviews each one of us at key points in the flow of work, and at the end of each interview he asks the same question, "What's your favorite sugaring story?" The show ends as I tell the camera that we've produced eighty-six gallons of pure Maine maple syrup in 1996, something more than a pint per taphole, an exemplary year.

Bill calls the movie *Life on Jackson Mountain*. He edits it to thirty-five minutes, and it's a hit. Beth and I show it to our friends. They love it. I take it to my weekly coffee group and show it between discussions of political and spiritual matters. They love it. I take it to work and show it to coworkers at lunch in the break room. They love it. The MMPA board asks to see it. I send a copy to a maple promotion affair in Virginia. The film is acclaimed—and lasting. The technology, however, the methods I describe, the processes I illustrate, are but a blip on a radar screen of sugaring technique, soon passé, archaic, a relic. I consign it to history and look for what's next.

The next change in technology comes quickly. Within a year, before the 1997 season begins, I learn that I'm likely the only commercial producer still taking down his tubing at the end of the season, washing it, and putting it back up the next year. The new washing style, I'm told, is to rinse the lines in place, pump a solution—5 percent Clorox in water is required by regulation—uphill through the lines and flush it out with plain water. So in 1997 I put my tubing in place to stay and rinse it at the end of the season, not by pumping, but by gravity. I lug the rinsing solution of Clorox and water up to the top of each tubing line and let the vacuum, assisted by my hand-operated plastic syrup pump, pull the solution through the lines. Instead of lugging tubing down and then up, I lug rinsing solution up. For me, the work is done faster, easier, and likely more effectively. A year or so later, however, I suffer a rodent attack that destroys many of the lines—so I go back to rinsing with plain water.

More change comes; this time environmental. I switch to a five-sixteenths-inch diameter spout, down from seven-sixteenths. The new spout is widely promoted by maple producers—spout manufacturers, too—following research at the Proctor Maple Research Center in Vermont. The bore hole is 28 percent less diameter than the traditional spout. The taphole's wall area is reduced the same percentage. Field trials at UVM's Proctor laboratory, however, indicate yields about the same as the larger spout when coupled with the use of vacuum. The benefit, Proctor assures us, comes from the smaller spout causing less damage to the sugar maple tree, thus protecting the tree's health. The lesser diameter drill bit carves out 28 percent less xylem than the larger spout. The taphole heals quicker; the tree grows faster.

I decide to change my syrup filter. Currently, I use a sixteen-inch-by-twenty-four-inch gravity-powered, flat felt filter lined with a paper prefilter. But the results are not consistent. Occasionally, I see a slight cloud, or haze. I'm selling a quantity of syrup in glass bottles now, as most producers are, and I can't risk a visible haze either in a glass bottle or in a crystal glass syrup pitcher displayed on a dining room table. I buy a filter press, a hand-operated plate and frame filter press, sometimes called a membrane filter press, which consists of several plates and frames assembled alternately to create a number of individual chambers where hot syrup, mixed with diatomaceous earth, is pressed through a membrane, leaving a cake of solids to be discarded. The plate and frame filter press is the most effective technique in syrup filtering available and puts a sparkle, folks say, in the syrup. The syrup's appearance, of course, will affect a customer's perception of quality. The press, I reason, will surely remove the last traces of the blasted cloud I occasionally encounter.

It happens. When I've installed the filter press and implemented the remaining post-video changes, my new and improved, almost self-operating, sap-gathering and boil-off processing system produces more syrup, sparkling in color and richer in taste. By 1999, I judge my syrup to be contest ready—clear, tasty, and right on grade—for any contest.

THE NORTH AMERICAN
MAPLE SYRUP COUNCIL

Contests are popular in the maple industry. Most every gathering of maple syrup producers prompts a contest. The Maine Maple Producers Association sponsors a syrup contest at its annual meeting in January. It has since the association came into existence in 1946. The annual Maple Festival and Sugaring-Off Party in Strong, during the few years of its existence, hosted a contest for Maine producers. Maple Mania, a summer convention in Maine of North American Maple Syrup Council members, hosts a contest. NAMSC and IMSI host a contest at their joint annual meeting, usually in the fall. In each contest, judges examine each entrant's sample and award points in each of four categories—density, clarity, taste, and grade—for the level of excellence attained. Producers of the top three scores in each grade receive swanky blue, white, and red ribbons. Best of Show receives an elegant pleated rosette. Producers all over Maine display their classy ribbons in their saphouse during the sap run, showing off what they make there.

In October 1999, the NAMSC will host their annual meeting, a three-day affair held jointly with the IMSI, in Portland, Maine. In March, seven months prior to the contest, I package a sample of my 1999 syrup production, seal it at 190°F, label it, store it in a freezer, and wait for the North American Maple Syrup Council to convene. The NAMSC contest is international. Producers from the maple-producing world—twelve states and four provinces—are eligible to enter. It's the major leagues of maple syrup contests. And it's my first competition since the appalling embarrassment I suffered in the 1967 MMPA contest at the Lewiston Armory—twelfth out of twelve entries. Since that humiliating event I have simply tried to produce a product satisfying to my customers. But I'm better at it now and inspired to have my syrup examined in a contest. I choose the most prestigious one of all, the NAMSC annual meeting.

The North American Maple Syrup Council has a long history. Founded originally as the National Maple Syrup Council, the NAMSC is an international network of maple-producing associations representing sixteen states and provinces in the United States and Canada. Formed in 1960 at Burton, Ohio, the council's mission is to bring together sugaring associations and industry leaders to learn and discuss common interests, experiences, and knowledge. The charter members—founders of the original National Maple Syrup Council—comprise the maple associations of six states: Massachusetts, New York, Ohio, Pennsylvania, Vermont, and Wisconsin.

The year following its founding, 1961, the Council met in Luxemburg, Wisconsin. Secretary Dorothy Zimmerman presented a proposed constitution and bylaws. The purpose of the organization, as described in its bylaws, was to promote research in the chemistry and technology of maple sap and the products developed from it. Such items as sugarbush management and disease control; markets and marketing of maple products; and standardization of maple syrup and spin-off uses without government regimentation have been on NAMSC's agenda. Competition among producers for the highest quality syrup, of course, fits its mission as well.

The highlight of the Luxemburg meeting in 1961, however, was the decision by the council to publish a newsletter. Vice Chairman Lloyd Sipple of New York agreed to proceed with publication, and in January 1962, Sipple, working alone without a budget, published the first issue of the *National Maple Syrup Digest*—known now as the *Maple Syrup*

Digest—and mailed a copy free of charge to more than six thousand known contacts.

Later, at a council meeting in Greenfield, Massachusetts, in 1964, the Maine Maple Producers Association applied for membership and became the ninth state association admitted to the National Maple Syrup Council, joining the original six and Michigan and New Hampshire, who were admitted in 1962. Maine producer Robert Smith of Skowhegan served as Maine's first representative to the council's board of directors. In 1989, the council, whose name by then had been changed to North American Maple Syrup Council, met for the first time in Maine, its thirtieth meeting hosted by MMPA in South Portland. Ten years later the council came back to Maine for its fortieth, this time in Portland.

The NAMSC arrives in Portland in October 1999. So does the International Maple Syrup Institute, a similar association of producers, packers, and maple equipment manufacturers formed in 1975 to promote and protect maple syrup and maple products. It's a joint meeting, perhaps three hundred people, more than one hundred maple syrup producers. It's the second time this group has been to Maine, and the MMPA, drawing on experience gained at the 1989 meeting in South Portland, puts on an exemplary show: a vendor's exhibit; a cadre of expert speakers; tours of downtown Portland and Casco Bay; a shopping trip to Maine's premier sporting goods store, L.L. Bean in Freeport; another shopping trek for the ladies to Freeport; a lobster and clam bake on House Island in Casco Bay; and a Saturday night banquet that overfills the Radisson Eastland's ballroom on Monument Square.

It's been seven months since I put the pint of medium amber syrup in my freezer. In October I retrieve it, wait for it to arouse from its coma, and deliver it to NAMSC for the judges to examine. Producers from eleven states and provinces are entered in the contest. The Vermonters are here, as are the Quebeckers, folks from the sugar district in Somerset County, and syrup-making experts from as far away as New York, Pennsylvania, and the New Brunswick outback. And many of Maine's expert maple syrup producers are in it, as well. But I am not intimidated. I know who I am, a small producer who does most of the work himself. But I'm in the game. Producers without syrup in the contest won't win for sure, or even finish second or third. Nor will most of us who are entered. But I'm calm; I know the odds; I'll accept what happens.

Maine producer Bob Moore, president of the MMPA, announces the results at the Saturday night banquet. Moore learned sugaring as a ten-year-old collecting sap for a neighbor who rewarded him with the last run for his own use. Moore boiled off his first batch of maple syrup in his mother's cake pan over a backyard cinder-block fireplace. Now he owns and runs Bob's Sugarhouse in Dover-Foxcroft, Maine, a five-thousand-taphole sugaring operation that ten years ago abandoned galvanized buckets in favor of vacuum-assisted plastic tubing, and now boils off syrup on a five-foot-by-fourteen-foot oil-fired Leader Revolution supplemented by a Steam-Away heat exchanger. Moore also has entered a sample of syrup in the contest.

Moore introduces himself and reads from information that's handed to him. He announces the results of the light amber category: Bruce Gillilan and Family from Saint Albans, Vermont, is first with 98 points. Girard's Sugarhouse from North Heath, Massachusetts, is winner in the medium amber category with 97 points. Tied for second place in the medium amber category with 96 points are Bruce Gillilan and Family of St. Albans, and Jackson Mountain Farm from Temple, Maine. "Who the hell is that?" Moore is heard to mutter into the microphone. I stand up. Moore keeps talking. "The Gillilan Family is awarded the second place ribbon," he announces. "Gillilan won a taste-off with Jackson Mountain for second. Third place ribbon goes to Jackson Mountain Farm."

Smiling ear to ear, I retrieve the ribbon from Moore. I don't hear anything else he says. I focus on my ribbon. Bonhomie Acres, Fredricktown, Ohio, I learn, wins dark amber. Bruce Gillilan and Family is awarded Best of Show for their light amber. Maine producers with high scores include Hall Farms East Dixfield second in the light amber category, and Bob's Sugarhouse Dover-Foxcroft fourth in light amber. I don't know anything else, just that Temple's sugar maples have just won an international ribbon for maple syrup excellence.

THE COMING OF
THE THIRD MILLENNIUM

Temple at the turn of the third millennium is a maple syrup mecca. Its hardwood forests and high topography are ideal for maple sugaring. Its settlers, the hill-farmers who came in the early 1800s, knew this and set aside their sugar maples for maple syrup as a sweetener and for topping. Their descendants, those who stayed on the place and protected and tapped the maples, continued the practice of backyard—or front yard or side yard—sugaring well into the twentieth century. I recall during my boyhood in the 1930s and 1940s seeing sugaring in the hills, not as a pastime but as necessary, as necessary as hunting game. In later years commercial sugaring, such as Jackson Mountain Farm, has appeared from time to time, as well. But not exclusively. The hill folks, the backyard and front yard and side yard folks, are there still, turning sugar maple sap into maple syrup for sweetener and topping.

In March 2001 Ken and Shirley Warren come to Temple from Vicksburg, Mississippi. The Warrens are retirees from work with the Mississippi State Highway Department. We—Beth and I—met them at a meeting of road administration officials in Charleston, West Virginia, in 1987. Ken headed the road building program in Mississippi, as I did in Maine. We talked the same language, albeit Ken's southern drawl was a bit more pronounced than my New England Yankee. I talked maple sugaring. He talked "blue ribbon cane see-rup." Now, curious about maple sugaring and anxious to see us again, Ken and Shirley "come up yonder," as Ken describes it, "Shirley wants to see the snow."

Temple is suffering from a snow-ladened March in 2001. Snow weighs heavy on the fields, deepest in years, close to four feet. Roadside snow, pushed up by the plow, blocks the view of the landscape. Snow plugs our driveway. It's everywhere. I shovel a twenty-inch wide pathway from our parking spot waist deep to the farmhouse, at least 150 feet. Ken and Shirley carry luggage up the pathway, as much luggage for a week as Beth and I brought in November for seven months. "Sap runnin' over yonder?" Ken asks me, as he trudges up the pathway wrestling with his ponderous load.

"I believe so," I answer. "Did yesterday, anyway."

We take them to the saphouse first, sitting behind Orchard Hill Road under its load of snow. The vacuum pump drones in a corner, while I show Ken the bit of sap it's bringing into the storage tank. Later in the afternoon, we come back and turn the run into four gallons of maple syrup. Big day for the Warren's, snow and syrup and all, and they want more.

Next morning we discover six more inches of snow on the top of what we had, and still coming down. The thermometer reads 10°F. Beth prepares a pancake breakfast. Shirley circles the interior of the farmhouse upstairs and down admiring the landscape out the frost-laden windows. "Unbelievable," she murmurs, and then again, "I don't believe it."

After breakfast, we tour Temple's outback in the Jeep, show off Temple's suburbia. Snow is still coming down, now building up some depth. We drive up Day Mountain Road, Temple's avenue of sugaring. A mile or so up, on the road to Santa Claus Lake, we stop at the corner with Lake Street. Steve—his last name is not generally known in Temple—a Pittsburg, Pennsylvanian who finds refuge in these woods and makes an annual trek here during sugaring season, has a fireplace and flat pan set up on his front lawn midst a scattering of sugar maples, perhaps twenty. Gallon-size plastic milk jugs full of frozen sap hang on the maples waiting for a warmer day. "Hardy tourists here," I tell Ken. "Maybe you and Shirley should look for a place 'round here, too."

Farther up Day Mountain Road, perhaps two miles, I turn left onto Kennison Road, badly rutted and full of falling snow. "Iffy going here," I mutter, as the Jeep slides off a deep rut into the roadside, and I yank it back onto the unplowed roadway. Ken turns on his video, and I stop in front of a circa 1830 farmhouse sporting a renovation in progress. A small pan of sap supported on an arch of rocks steams over a fire. A barking dog charges the Jeep, and a shouting woman follows. Ken rolls down his window. "You makin' see-rup?" he asks.

The woman, Kathy Dorr, who was brought up in Temple and moved to the old Kennison place some years ago when she married John, shushes the dog and hollers, "Not too much, cold as it is. Sap is frozen anyway."

"How much you make in a yee-ah?"

"Barely enough to get through," she says.

We chat a few minutes while Ken defends himself against the friendly dog. "You make it every year?" I ask her.

"Sure do. I need it. I've got ice everywhere in these pans now, but I'll turn it into maple syrup when the weather warms."

Back on Day Mountain Road, the snow still coming down, I turn left and drive farther up, stop at the Schanz place. The Schanzes, Gene and Jo-Ann, the Saturday postmaster in the village post office, live back a bit from the road, and Gene has wisely cleared the land in the front— southeast—side of the house, cleared out all but the sugar maples, and fashioned a barrel stove, a flat pan, and a roof covering it all into a boiling rig, midst his thirty or so sugar maples. It's quiet here, sounds are muffled by the snow. Buckets hang passive against the trees; a few covers shelter yesterday's sap. We move on, turn around at Jackson Mountain Road, and retreat through our own tracks, now half full of snow, to Intervale Road, which is plowed. We turn left toward the village.

Ken Dunham has a place on the bank of Hen Mitchell Brook. A bit of steam is rising off a flat pan perched on a barrel-stove arch, likely has been all day. No one around. "The fire will go out before the sap is gone," I tell Ken. "Then, if it's not syrup he'll save it, put with yesterday's, which is likewise half done, and finish it all off later." I drive on and we come to Ron Smith's place on Farmington Road. I stop and explain what I see:

"Smith is a large-size producer as backyard sugaring goes. He taps trees here, and at his daughter's across town, and out on Porter Hill as well. Puts in about sixty spouts; boils off the syrup right there in his shed," I point out, "on a manufactured arch and a small commercial flat-pan evaporator. He sits inside with a coffee pot and a book—and dry wood—and fires the arch without having to stand up. Makes about twelve gallons a year. No license required, longs he's under fifteen gallons and doesn't sell any of it. Shares it with family and friends all over town. After the season's over," I tell Ken, "Ron's sap shed becomes Ron's tool shed—until next March.

We turn right. A mile up Varnum Pond Road, I stop in front of Erald Farmer's place. Plastic tubing is strung along the road beside us and into a field along a stone wall. A saphouse sits on the opposite side about a hundred yards away. Vents in the roof are closed. "Farmer is licensed to produce maple syrup commercially," I tell Ken. "Maybe two or three hundred tapholes, whatever his kids feel up to doing. They collect sap in a pickup truck with a tank in the back," I say, "and transport it to the small saphouse you see over there, where he boils it in what Leader calls a pint-size evaporator. Sells most of it for cash out of his pizza shop in Farmington."

I turn right onto Orchard Hill Road. Snow is heavy in the road again. Must be eight or nine inches total. I stop in front of David Stevens's and point to his boiling setup, fireplace and flat pan behind his house. "Stevens," I say, "taps in his backyard, boils off what syrup he needs for himself in a flat pan there, and then he brings any extra sap over to me, dumps it in a barrel I leave in front of the saphouse. I pay him with half the syrup I make from it—or cash if he wants. I have two other similar arrangements, as well. John Ernst, whose place is on Farmer Road over behind Varnum Pond, also produces syrup in his backyard. In a good sap year, when his rig can't keep up with it, he transports the surplus over to Jackson Mountain Farm—for half the syrup as well. And the Nicholas kids on Maple Street downtown: Elizabeth, Tucker, and Ben tap the one-hundred-year-old sugar maples on their front lawn and collect the sap into a five-gallon container. I pick it up daily when the sap's running and boil it off. They earn enough syrup to last the family nearly the whole year. It's a tradition not uncommon in Temple's history."

In the shelter of the farmhouse for lunch—as it will turn out, for the rest of the day—we tell Ken and Shirley what we've seen through the snowstorm: eight backyard, side yard, and front yard sugaring sites in Temple alone, where maple syrup is produced not just because it's fun—it is, of course—but because it's needed. And those eight places likely do not include everyone. "It's the culture here," I tell Ken. "I don't know another small town like it."

A year later, the fall of 2002, Beth and I drive to Vicksburg, Mississippi, and help Ken and Shirley with the cotton harvest, as it were. Ken doesn't raise cotton anymore since he left the family place. But he did so in his youth, and Shirley too, worked in the fields with the family and the hired crew picking by hand the annual crop. Now he's promised to deliver us a cotton field where we'll get our chance at the backbreaking work. But first, he takes us to Brandon, an historic old Mississippi town of 1,500 people fifty years ago, brick courthouse on the square and all that, where Ken was raised on the family place.

His granddaddy's farm, in addition to an acre of cotton and a large vegetable garden, produced sorghum then from blue ribbon cane. Blue ribbon syrup, they called it, produced from cane squeezings boiled in a flat pan, much the same process as boiling off maple syrup in Maine. The squeezings, a somewhat murky liquid of heavier consistency than maple sap, come from running cane stalks through a cane mill turned by a mule. Ken's summer job as a teenager, he tells me, was "to get up early and have the boiler full of cane juice by the time Grandpa Irvin finished breakfast." The production team—Ken, Grandpa Irvin, and the mule—"made molasses from blue ribbon cane for the folks in rural Brandon, and kept one gallon out of every four for the toll." When Ken went off to Mississippi State University in 1958, he tells me, "The mule retired, and Daddy started using a tractor and a power take-off to turn the mill."

On the outskirts of Brandon we find Grandpa Irvin's somewhat dilapidated boiling shack. It's no longer producing blue ribbon cane syrup. His old flat pan, about eight inches deep with a tin bottom and wooden sides, sits askew an arch made of bricks, testimony to when Brandon survived on its own, before being overrun by urban sprawl and made into a dependent suburbia of Mississippi's capitol city, Jackson. Finding that old pan was a step back in time for me, and Ken as well. And he vowed to make another trip to Temple, "up yonder," he grinned, "an' help squeeze the sap outta the sugar maples again."

The 2003 season opens for Beth and me on television. On March 4, a Tuesday, we go to Portland's Public Market with Bob Smith, Al Bolduc, Lyle Merrifield, Ben McKenney, and other MMPA members and spouses for the taping of Jim Crocker's WB 51 cooking show, *The Maine Dish*. We comprise the television audience. For us, it's the unofficial opening of the maple syrup season.

We watch Crocker and chef Norm Hebert of York County Technical College simmer maple-marinated scallops and maple-basted ribs, and bake a maple syrup pie for the curious eyes of the WB 51 camera crew circling the makeshift studio. TV audiences will see the show on March 16 and 20. Chef Hebert has promised us, once the filming is over, we'll have a taste of everything. "Crisp up the bacon there, Norm. It's so-o-o-o sweet," Crocker instructs.

Hebert tends to the syrupy ribs and bacon-wrapped scallops. Crocker hypes the impending Maine Maple Sunday while he whisks up a maple syrup pie, one, he says, that will "knock your socks off." Tom Hansen, the Public Market's wine pundit, suggests a Napa Valley Chardonnay. The studio audience—that's us—contributes light applause and waits for the tasting.

Following the filming, Chef Hebert, as he said he would, shares the food with the audience. The spare ribs, though not my favorite food, seem improved sufficiently by the syrup for them to be suitable for eating, and the pie, sumptuous as it is, tastes close to the flavor of Georgia's pecan pie. Smith and Bolduc eat the scallops before Hebert can serve them to any of the other guests.

On March 6 I'm in Yarmouth convinced that it's still too breezy and cold for tapping trees. Beth and I drive to Augusta and the MMPA Board of Directors meeting at the Farm Bureau office. Bob Smith, in his second—or third or fourth—term as president, and the only Maine maple producer in history to be elected to the Maple Hall of Fame, presides. First item is the governor's First Tap ceremony. "Do we have a firm date yet?" Smith asks. "Will the governor be there? Does he know about it? Has anyone heard from Deanne Herman? Should we use the Ag Commissioner instead?"

Al Bolduc, quick-witted, grayed, loud, talkative, and a survivor of the early skiing on Sugarloaf Mountain and who now produces about forty barrels of maple syrup each year and promotes Somerset County sugaring beyond reason, speaks, "Maybe we should have a new venue for the first tap," he says. "Say Somerset County."

I speak up then, trying to balance Bolduc's emphasis on upstate Somerset County. "Why not Southern Maine?" I ask. "It might be warm enough there not to have to stomp your feet all the time. And I'd suggest we use a personality instead of the governor. How about a weatherman? Kevin Mannix, say? Maybe he'd stop talking up Vermont maple syrup on the evening weather report."

Joe Suga, an equipment dealer in Vassalboro who also taps perhaps two hundred maple trees, laughs. Smith bangs his gavel and speaks again, "But the thing takes an hour and a half, and then we have come back to the Ag Show on the 29th in the rotunda."

Jeremy Steeves, an upscale Skowhegan producer and packer who markets his syrup in New York City and is often late when the directors meet because he's being interviewed by the *New York Times*, ends the discussion, "I'll tell Deanne we want it on the same day as the Ag Show."

Smith leafs through a handful of committee reports: a grant application, the impending newsletter, status of subchapters, the website, and then stops. "Now," he says, "Maine Maple Sunday. We've got a new Maple Sunday flyer here, but it's late. How come? We should get this stuff out sooner. Increase our coverage. Get free radio exposure. And we should keep our Ag focus going. Maybe come up with some roadside promotion for the fall too?"

Bolduc again: "All the eastern states are copying us on Maine Maple Sunday. We should make it two days . . . or a week . . . or they'll be tapping our tree."

The meeting goes on.

Finally, Bolduc has an action item for the Board. He hands Smith a letter. "This is from the Somerset Sugarmakers," he tells Smith. "They're asking for approval of subchapter status. How soon can you take action?" Bolduc is pressing for recognition of the Somerset County Sugarmakers Association. But the MMPA board has been slow to approve previous requests.

"Did you include your bylaws?" I ask.

"No."

"Send them to me," says Smith.

"Write me a letter and ask for them. Then I'll send them," and so it goes. Somerset County will eventually get the recognition it deserves. But in the meantime the board obliges itself to only the duties required by Article V of the bylaws, duties "usually pertaining to such offices." Bolduc waits. A week later Deanne Herman, head of the Marketing Division at the Maine Department of Agriculture, notifies Smith of Governor Baldicci's preferred date for the First Tap ceremony. The event is scheduled for March 19 at 9:30 a.m. on the lawn of the Blaine House in Augusta, home of Maine's governors and their families since 1920, where a single maple tree stands and waits.

The First Tap ceremony, 1998, was also held at the Blaine House. Angus King was governor. Deanne Hermann was new with the MDOA's marketing group. I suspect the ceremony was her idea. She called me first, described what she wanted to do, and asked me to find a suitable maple tree somewhere on the state house grounds. I discovered it on the side lawn of the Blaine House. She did the remaining work, including getting Governor King's approval to tap the tree and hype Maine maple syrup on Blaine House property in front of a cadre of TV cameras and reporters.

Governor King showed up on time for the ceremony wearing an iconic Maine lumberjack's red checkered shirt and L.L. Bean boots. He sought a bit of advice selecting a location for the hole, then drilled it and hung the bucket. King loved tapping that tree and would eventually, during his tenure as governor, tap it five times.

But it's cold in Augusta on March 19, 2003. Cold everywhere. No sap. No syrup. No producer in Maine, except possibly in York County, has made any maple syrup. Too cold. The First Tap ceremony on the Blaine House lawn is set for 9:30 a.m. By nine o'clock, three TV news photographers huddle around their tripods, the Maine Maple Producers Association has fashioned an outdoor display of maple syrup and candy, and Eric Ellis has set up a hot stove on a table next to the state's most famous maple tree, ready to make maple taffy. A mixed contingent of reporters, journalists, cameramen, state employees on coffee break, and a sample of Maine's producers begin to wander the grounds, rub their hands together, and make small talk with each other. Robert Speer, commissioner of Agriculture, comes. Also Deputy Commissioner Ned Porter, and marketing specialist Deanne Herman.

Governor John Baldacci shows up some ten minutes early. I introduce myself as vice president of the association, and Eric Ellis and Joe Suga as MMPA directors. Baldacci smiles and uses his ten minutes to work the crowd. At 9:30 I pass him the brace and bit. "We're ready when you are, Governor."

Baldacci stares at the crank-shaped "thingamajig" he calls it, and then turns to me, "Do you have any instructions?"

"Actually, Governor," I answer, "Commissioner Speer is your agricultural expert. I think he can guide you through this."

"Who, me? Not me," Speer blurts. "It's been too-oo long a time since I tapped a tree."

I lean toward the governor and say, "Just drill a hole about two inches deep with that thing, and then hammer in the spout. I won't let you do anything wrong."

Baldacci finds a spot and starts turning the drill. After about a dozen revolutions he looks at me. "How'm I doin'?" he asks.

"Doing great, Governor," says Speer, who has already admitted he doesn't know how himself.

Baldacci glances at me again. "How come I'm not making a hole?"

"The bit may be wobbling a tad too much," I tell him. "Try holding it a dite steadier."

He finishes the hole, taps in the spout, and hangs the MMPA bucket. I hand him a cover.

"What's this?" he asks.

"Goes on top," I say. "Keeps the snow and rain out."

He grins. "First time I ever tapped a tree."

"You did fine, Governor."

The 2003 season produces thirty gallons of syrup. I don't know what happened. Sap runs first on March 22 and last on April 14, three weeks. During the three weeks, we boil off six batches of syrup. Our biggest batch is six gallons—twice. Our smallest is zero—fifteen times. Following the three-week trickle, I rinse the tubing, wash the evaporator, lock the saphouse door, and try to figure what happened.

Chapter Twenty-One

BACTERIA WARS

I figure the 2003 disaster comes from bacteria. The curse of maple sugaring is back. The sealed tubing network and vacuum in the lines, such as we enjoyed when the tubing was new, have kept the incessant microbe noticeably away from the taphole for ten or so years. But with the coming of the 1990s, though we still produced about a pint of syrup per taphole, the tubing started to show its age.

The aging, I suspect, was accelerated by multiple causes. I haven't taken the tubing down to clean for several years. And I eliminated the required 5 percent Clorox rinse a few years ago when I noticed the tubing gnawed and shredded by squirrels, moles, and mice attracted to the salty residue, creating immeasurable work for me repairing and replacing the remnants. I rinse tubing in place now with plain water and leave it strung tree to tree to face the ravages of winter. The old DeLavel, too, has aged. It leaks considerable oil, and its customary output of vacuum is now something less than 6 inHg, rendering it virtually ineffective.

I need about five and a half gallons of sap out of a taphole to make a pint of syrup. Five and a half gallons is about the maximum I can expect from pole trees with fewer leaves, smaller leaves, and 2 percent sugar in the sap. But in 2003 I'm not getting five and a half gallons, I'm getting about three gallons. Bacteria are healing the tapholes, cutting off the sap runs, and shortening the season. Syrup production, of course, declines as well. Instead of a pint of syrup per taphole, I'm making a bit more than a half-pint. I need to fix that, bring the sap yield back up.

To keep the holes fresh, I have access to the same myriad of ineffective options that I've already suffered, and that producers before me have suffered also. Reaming the holes midseason is one, though I see reaming of less value than the required investment in time and energy. The paraformaldehyde pellet is another, but only at great risk to the sugar maples. The pellet is also banned, regulated, and classified as a pesticide, unavailable to those without an applicator's license, which is impossible for a sugarmaker to acquire. Replacing tubing lines, a new start, so to speak, is also an option. And so is doing nothing.

Of the options, higher vacuum—25 inHg—is touted by producers. I'm told high vacuum will increase sap yields. But I don't adopt 25 inHg. I'm a small producer, and I don't see the benefit justifying the additional cost. I am aware, however, that a change in my vacuum system is long overdue. I switch out the ancient DeLavel, which is now in its third millennium of use and has barely produced 6 inHg for a few years now, and install a new Conde, said to remove enough air from the tubing network—8 CFM @ 16 inHg—to increase the sap yield to about 5.5 gallons per taphole, a pint of syrup, perfect for my eight-hundred-taphole grove, and a 100 percent improvement from the paltry performance of the DeLavel. I've now progressed back to 1991. But I'm still not satisfied. I know I can produce more sap.

The DeLavel was given to me years ago by my friend Wes Kinney, who found it in a barn in Knox, a generous move on his part and an extremely beneficial one for me. The one-hundred-year-old DeLavel seemed state of the art then, and for more than twenty-five years I have listened to it clank away in the back corner of my sugar shack and watched the sap level rise on a gauge next to the storage tank. And on days the sap didn't run, I traveled to Osgood's farm shop in East Dixfield, or to Jim Zahner's barn in Fairfield Center, and brought more vacuum pump oil to Temple to glut that thirsty pump. But Wes was right in 1978 when he said the pump would treat me right. The old DeLavel served me well. But I'm tired of cleaning up after it and need more performance. The Conde will—somehow—take me there.

Maple syrup producers have struggled with bacterial contamination of the taphole for many years. As early as 1983, research into contaminated tapholes by the Proctor Maple Research Center at the University of Vermont targeted tubing systems for a solution. Mariafranca Morselli and William King, researchers at the University of Vermont, discovered that microbial biofilms develop on the interior walls of tubing systems with time. As tubing ages, the biofilm will, they wrote, grow and eventually restrict or clog the flow of sap. Morselli knew the problem was bacteria—*Pseudomonas geniculata*—the blight of high sap yields. And so did the bucket and spout producers of the last century know, though perhaps they didn't use the Latin to describe it, that premature healing of the taphole shuts down most sap-gathering operations midseason and forces producers to ream their tapholes to salvage a full crop. Tim Perkins at Vermont's Proctor Center also knew that the use of vacuum in tubing systems did not eliminate bacteria. Vacuum actually worsened the problem, Perkins alleged, by creating negative pressure within the tree, and causing sap, when a vacuum leak occurs or vacuum is shut down, to surge backward into the trees carrying a plethora of bacteria directly into the tapholes.

In 2007, Perkins and others at the Proctor Center sought the prevention of bacteria migration into tapholes. They set out to develop a spout that would prevent backflow of sap, some type of check that would prevent reverse flow when negative pressure disappeared from the lines. Perkins searched for a commercially available control, or a similar device, that he could adapt to sap flow. Finding nothing, he switched to development of one himself, a new and unique replaceable insert for the stubby spout. Stubby spout replaceable inserts—without a check—had been developed earlier and paired with stubby spouts to allow the insert, which is the only part of the spout in contact with the tree, to be discarded and replaced annually. The disposable insert, however, failed to protect the taphole from backflow and became just another failed attempt to control bacteria.

Undaunted by the failure, Perkins placed a small plastic ball as a check valve within a modified insert. The ball, which acted as a shutoff, prevented negative pressure in the tree from drawing sap out of the tubing when vacuum in the lines disappeared for any reason. In the spring of 2008, Proctor and the Leader Evaporator Company conducted chamber testing, a controlled laboratory experiment on a prototype check-valve adapter, Perkins called it. The check-valve adapter produced 26 percent more sap than the control, a standard plastic spout. Microbial contamination of the check-valve adapter measured only 30 percent of the control. The Proctor Center and Leader applied for a patent.

Testing continued into 2009. Again, the Proctor Center and Leader collaborated in field testing a commercial version of a check-valve adapter, one that would be adaptable to annual replacement. Two separate trials were conducted. The research found that with new check-valve adapters and new drop lines, sap yield increased as much as 60 percent, a figure unexpectedly high. Perkins described the result as "comparable to those achieved using paraformaldehyde pellets." Leader and Proctor agreed that the replaceable check-valve adapter concept would also work well in practice. Perkins, in his October 2009 research report, stated that "systems employing replaceable check-valve adapters should produce more sap than systems without them."

U.S. Senator Patrick Leahy announced Proctor's check-valve adapter development—a high-production spout he called it—to the media. Perkins at Proctor Center, Leahy reported, expected the spout to extend the sugaring harvest three weeks, prevent sap from flowing uphill, and boost syrup yields 90 percent. The word spread. Gary Gaudette, president of the Leader Evaporator Company, predicted a "revolutionary impact" on the maple industry. Leader's Bruce Gillilan ordered three million spouts from the manufacturer, Vermont's Progressive Plastics Company, to sell in the United States and Canada during the coming season, and Senator Leahy—Leahy reportedly secured federal funds for the spout's research and development—proclaimed that manufacturer Progressive Plastics had added two work shifts at their plant in Williston, Vermont, to meet the demand.

On Orchard Hill in 2009, I read this news with a bit of skepticism. The Proctor Maple Research Center is good at what they do, I know. Given direction and a loose leash, Proctor can perhaps eliminate a worldwide recession or conquer global warming, but when it comes to doubling the maple sap yield, I'm a skeptic—and I admit it. I have tinkered with bacteria for years. Bacteria's damage to the sap run is incalculable, perhaps unsolvable. Though I'm a skeptic, I'm also realistic. The Mainer in me says not to burn all my bridges.

I have seen too much evidence of the pesky microbes, lost too much sap to sealed tapholes, and spent too much time trying to outwit the ornery pest to disregard even a miracle cure. I've experienced ideal sap conditions when I couldn't explain why the sap didn't run; seasons of only one normal sap run, followed by but a dribble; seasons that yielded less sap every day and lasted but two weeks; and seasons that for some reason ended in mid-March midst ideal pendulum temperatures. I need to rid Orchard Hill of that wretched microbe. If a tiny plastic ball can revolutionize the syrup industry, boost job creation, drive economic development, add weeks to the sap season, and create a syrup bonanza, I'm all for it. I call Gwen Kinney at Kinney Maple Supplies in Thorndike and ask her to send me two hundred replaceable check-valve adapters and the companion stubbies. I figure these two hundred adapters could mean a 40 percent increase in my syrup production, enough to notice whether Proctor's adapter actually makes a difference.

In January 2009 at the Maine Agricultural Trade Show, I watch Bruce Gillilan showcase the backflow effects of vacuum in a chamber he has put together for the show. Gillilan cuts the vacuum, and water flows backward out of tubing and up a dropline into the sealed chamber, presumably carrying the persistent microbe. I'm impressed—and stimulated. I seize the bag of check-valve adapters Mary Ann Kinney has brought me from Kinney Maple Supplies and head straight away for Orchard Hill in Temple. Time has arrived, I mutter, to find out whether a microbe barrier will yield more sap—or not.

On Orchard Hill, I replace two hundred of my five hundred bacteria-contaminated spouts with the high-tech replaceable check-valve adapter and stubby, presumably cutting off the backflow of sap into the taphole in a considerable portion—40 percent—of the tubing network. I discard a hundred or so aged and grubby drop lines and replace them with new and clean drops. When that is done, Joe Hodgkins, the thirty-something son of former partner Bill Hodgkins and a protégé now at Jackson Mountain Farm, proposes adding two hundred new tapholes farther up the hill using new, bacteria-free tubing, droplines, and spouts, all intended to increase syrup production.

Joe came to see me in 2006, wanted to "learn maple syrup." He had been away from Temple since high school, studied several years at the University of Montana, and left there without a degree in 2004 or so, but not without the learning. He followed a girlfriend to Kansas and, when that didn't work out, he kept moving. He worked agriculture in Costa Rica for a winter and then came back to Temple. The past year or two has been spent cooperative gardening—food production—in both Maine and Costa Rica. I invite him to come along with me.

Joe fits at Jackson Mountain Farm. He knows food. He adds brains, energy, and muscle to the work we do here. And he absorbs all the learning I offer. When he proposes adding tapholes to the network from his dad's piece up the hill, I don't hesitate. I tell him the truth. "Joe," I answer, "I've been up there. It's hard, and I'm not going back, not on my own. But I'll help you."

We climb up beyond my property line onto Bill's and fashion a plan of what he'd like to do. We go back later and put up a wire. On the wire we fashion new mainline plastic pipe, tubing, drop lines, and spouts far enough up the hill to extend the plastic network about two hundred spouts. When tapping time comes in February, nearly 60 percent of the Orchard Hill bush—now more than seven hundred tapholes—is free of microbial contamination at the taphole.

So, what happens? Does the experiment work? Are the results favorable? How does it all come out? Well, I don't know exactly. I don't compile scientific documentation in my saphouse: standard deviations, percentile equivalents, probability densities, variance analyses, or any of that. Instead, I tap the trees early, though perhaps not early by Jeremy Steeves's standards—Steeves, a fifth-generation producer at the family-owned Strawberry Hill Farms in Skowhegan, starts tapping New Year's Day, drills eighteen thousand tapholes alone, and finishes barely before the first run, usually in February—yet early by Jackson Mountain Farm's standards. This year, driven to get all the sap that comes to us, Joe and I tap out on February 16. Then we wait—and watch. At the first sign of a sap run, I turn the vacuum on and leave it on.

We boil sap first on February 18, last on March 16, and most every day in between. At the end of the first week in March, the two hundred tapholes with check-valve adapters, the two-hundred-taphole extension up the hill with new tubing, and the one hundred tapholes with new drop lines are still producing sap, plenty of sap. But hardly a trickle remains from the spouts that had seen previous duty. By March 20, a bit more than four weeks after the first run, the check-valve adapters are the only source of moisture I observe on the hillside. The nights have warmed, and not even the revolutionary adapter produces running sap. It is over.

Does bacteria-proofing make a difference? Yes, it does. The hill produces a record 80 percent more syrup per taphole in 2009 than the previous five-year average. This is a significant result, and contrary to what statisticians are claiming: a low-yield season in Maine. So who should get the credit for all this syrup? Who do I thank for the big sap runs I've harvested? The researchers, I say. The Proctor Maple Research Center and the Leader Evaporator Company.

The Proctor Maple Research Center was the first permanent maple research facility to establish in America. It opened in 1946 in an eight-foot-by-twelve-foot shed located on a former two-hundred-acre hill farm in Underhill Center, Vermont. Maple research into effective sap collection, efficient evaporation, and maple syrup quality improvement, started at once and continues even now. Since 1946, the original Proctor shed, an arm of the Vermont Agricultural Experiment Station, has expanded to an eight-thousand-square-foot research laboratory, a 1,400-taphole sugar bush, a modern sugar shack, and sundry outbuildings and equipment. Its mission is the same as when it started: research, demonstration, and education.

Over the years the Proctor research team has delved into sap flow rates, maple physiology, economics, and such worrisome bones as contamination, metabolism, combustion efficiencies, and the effects on maple tree growth of acid rain, the pear thrip, and fertilization. It has looked into sap chemistry, studied flow rates from small tapholes, and evaluated the effects of air injection and other advanced technologies on the flavor and quality of maple syrup. Recent publications have centered on efficient tubing layouts, effective tapping dates, high-yield vacuum systems, cleanliness, and eliminating bacterial constraint of sap flow. It was Dr. Tim Perkins and his folks at Proctor who discovered the need for the replaceable check-valve adapter and produced an effective prototype.

Many of the findings and recommendations of maple research at Proctor are being applied—or should be—in every progressive sugarbush and saphouse in Maine. Producers, packers, dealers, consumers, and, I suspect, bankers benefit from Proctor's work. The industry reciprocates by contributing money for more research. Producers, dealers, associations, and friends of maple donate cash to the North American Maple Syrup Council's research fund. The Maine Maple Producers Association, for example, makes an annual generous donation from its war chest to the NAMSC for maple research. I expect many other state maple associations do the same, or more.

As an indicator of the value of Proctor's research, its sugarbush in Underhill Center produces 0.6 gallons—nearly five pints—of maple syrup per taphole. And the Proctor site is on the National Register of Historic Places. It should also be listed in the current volume of *Guinness World Records*.

During the next two years, Jackson Mountain Farm finishes its conversion to the replaceable check-valve adapter on all its tapholes, as well as a routine change of one hundred drop lines each year. Orchard Hill is sated with tiny plastic balls, more than seven hundred. In 2011 we produce 145 gallons of maple syrup, 1.6 pints per taphole. It costs us thirty-five cents per taphole, to double our production. Hopefully we have won the fight with the miserable *Pseudomonas geniculata*. I'm moving forward. I have other things to do.

Chapter Twenty-Two

HYDROMETERS, HYDROTHERMS, AND WOODEN CHIPS

Award of the third-place ribbon in the 1999 NAMSC international maple syrup contest begins a period of syrup-producing excellence at Jackson Mountain Farm. During the next decade, we accumulate eight more ribbons—three blue, three red, and two white—all signifying the high-quality syrup being made on Orchard Hill, clearly a step upward from our dismal beginnings.

The first ribbon comes barely three months after the shocker in Portland. In January 2000 I take a pint of light amber maple syrup out of the freezer and submit it to the MMPA's annual contest in Augusta. It comes from a batch made a week previous to syrup I made for the Portland contest. The judges award us 92 points, and Jackson Mountain Farm wins the coveted blue ribbon, its first. Hall Farms, a seven-thousand-taphole sugaring endeavor in East Dixfield, where Rodney Hall boasts that Hall Farms offers "the best tasting, highest quality Maine maple syrup," wins a blue ribbon for medium amber. First prize for dark amber goes to Maine Maple Products in Madison. Hall Farms, however, measures up to Rodney's braggadocio and is named Best of Show.

Year after year, we face strong competition for an MMPA statewide ribbon, and we strive to be competitive. The following year, 2001, we win another blue ribbon, taking first place for dark amber at the January show in Augusta. Four ribbons now hang from our bulletin board at the saphouse. In 2003, however, our sample scores the minimum 20 points for density, and we go home with a total of 84 points and no ribbon. But in 2005 we score again. Our medium amber wins second place. And in 2006 our dark amber syrup scores 97 points, a perfect 30 points for density, and we manage second place again, our sixth ribbon in seven years.

Syrup density is critical to superior syrup. Contest judges award additional points for density values close to the standard 66° Brix and fewer points for values that wander toward the periphery of the permissible: 65.1° Brix and 68.9° Brix. Judges use refractometers to measure density, a precise instrument that, it's said, is accurate to within 0.2° Brix. I'm sure this level of accuracy attracts producers to use a refractometer in the saphouse; a refractometer offers a better chance at a perfect score.

I've never used a refractometer, and I suspect I never will. I don't need the kind of accuracy that comes with multiple digits following the decimal point. Actually, the refractometer may not be what it is professed to be anyway. Its accuracy is only within 0.2° Brix, and it's not well suited for measuring the density of hot syrup. Though this variation may seem somewhat immaterial, given the scale of accuracy we work with—I use a hydrotherm—I'm motivated to wonder just how well a refractometer actually performs in practice.

In 2007 I submit two samples of the same batch of syrup to the MMPA contest, where a judge measures density with a refractometer. I do this because I cannot reliably determine the grade of the batch with a color comparator. I don't know whether it is medium amber or light amber grade. Both samples look the same to me, so I submit one sample labeled medium and one labeled light to the contest, knowing that one will be rejected for grade. The results are telling—and surprising. As measured by the contest judge, density values of the two samples differ by 1.5° Brix, and both samples are rejected, one for grade and one for density. The wide variation in density surprises me. I presume the judge determined the density of both samples using the same refractometer, reputed to be the most precise of the density measuring instruments, accurate to within 0.2° Brix. But my two samples of the same syrup differ by 1.5° Brix.

The earliest instrument used to measure density of maple syrup was likely a wooden spoon—or a wooden chip. The cook would dip it in the boiling syrup and watch the hot liquid drip off the edge. If it came off in sheets—or aproned—it was finished, the right consistency, the correct weight per unit volume, a sugar content high enough to be spoil-proof. Later, when maple syrup was defined as maple sap that boils at 219.1°F, a thermometer became popular. Both instruments—and others—are still commonly used.

Maine maple syrup producers—non-Mainers, as well—have several options available to determine the density of maple syrup. A simple candy thermometer is one. A syrup hydrometer, a hydrotherm, and a refractometer are others. A blow test is another. To conduct a blow test, the boiler ties a supple twig into a loop and dips it into the boiling syrup. When he catches a film in the loop and can blow bubbles through it, the syrup is done. And more options exist. Pick your poison. None are absolutely accurate. All involve a moving target, though an experienced and attentive cook, one who has the advantage of years of practicing, can produce satisfactory syrup just by observing how it sheets off a scoop, or by the character of the boiling foam next to the draw, as his father and grandfather did before him. But it's best to have an instrument, particularly if the syrup will be for sale—or entered in a contest. Any choice used carefully and prudently and with consideration for its limitations—some methods are more consistent and accurate than others—will produce reasonable results; that is, close enough.

Many producers consider the hydrometer, first used in the 1800s, the most reliable. And it's likely the most popular as well, commonly used by virtually all large commercial producers, producers who market bulk syrup and producers who buy bulk syrup and package it for retail sale. Though claimed by some to be the only certified instrument for measuring the density of maple syrup, the hydrometer is calibrated for syrup temperatures of 60°F and 211°F, temperatures only seldom seen in a saphouse. At any other syrup temperature a hydrometer reading must be corrected for the actual temperature of the syrup, resulting in a complex and time-consuming procedure to accurately determine the density of syrup being made.

On the other hand, the Ayres hydrotherm, invented in the 1930s by Henry Fairfax Ayres of Addison, Vermont, a graduate of the U.S. Military Academy at West Point in 1908, employs a column of red liquid that indicates the point—bottom of the red liquid meniscus—at which syrup is at standard Brix at any syrup temperature. No need to calibrate it. Just wait thirty seconds for the red column to adjust to the syrup's temperature. The hydrotherm should float in the hot syrup at the top of the red column. Ayres, however, calibrated his hydrotherm at 65.8° Brix, a dite under Maine's standard of 66.0° Brix. But a bit of target practice with Colonel Ayres's hydrotherm will reveal to the producer where the top of the liquid column should show for standard grade Maine syrup. Experienced producers defend the hydrotherm as a simple, quick, and a consistently accurate device at any temperature.

A hand-held refractometer also seems relatively simple to operate. Place a drop of syrup on a small window at one end and, viewing through the eyepiece, read the density on a calibrated background scale on the other. The refractometer corrects for syrup temperature automatically before revealing a reading, a considerably convenient feature. Refractometers, however, NAMSC writes in its producers' manual, are expensive, require periodic recalibration with a substance of known density—oil is common—and are not well suited to measuring the density of hot syrup, since a drop of hot syrup can give off a relatively sizeable amount of water by evaporation in the short time taken to conduct the measurement, which, of course, would skew the results.

I own an Ayres hydrotherm. Purchased it for $7 in 1964. I bought a backup a few years later for $9, but I still use the original hydrotherm. Yes, I know that other supposedly more accurate density-measuring devices—the syrup hydrometer and refractometer—are available for producers, even recommended, but I'm not persuaded to use one. I use an Ayres hydrotherm to test my syrup for standard density, and a maple syrup contest to validate the results.

Sometime back in the 1970s, a mild hullaboo came up over the accuracy of the hydrotherm. Its detractors alleged it uncertified. As a consequence of that controversy, I bought a syrup hydrometer, which was then—and is now—the only instrument said to be certified to measure the density of maple syrup. The hydrometer came with a calibration sheet for temperature correction, stamped with the notation, "certified in Vermont." *What the hell good is this?* I thought. *Why would I want this thing?* Vermont requires a higher Brix value for standard density syrup than Maine does.

Nevertheless, I give the Vermont-certified hydrometer a try. And within a month I break it hurrying to get the hang of an accurate reading before the syrup temperature drops another degree. But I'm not discouraged over the loss of my so-called certified hydrometer. I just toss the pieces and go back to what works for me, my old and reliable hydrotherm.

In 2009 the NAMSC annual meeting and maple syrup contest is scheduled for Maine again, this time in Bar Harbor. I package two pints of dark amber syrup in April and put them in my freezer. My objective is to verify the quality of my syrup—and obtain another reading on the accuracy and consistency of a refractometer vis-à-vis an Ayres hydrotherm. I enter one of the samples in the NAMSC contest and then, not having any other reason to attend the gala, stay away from Bar Harbor and wait for the results to be mailed. I reason the contest results will be the same whether I'm there or not. Soon I learn that I scored 96 points out of a possible 100. Density is 67.0° Brix, a full point above Maine's minimum acceptable density, almost perfect. But no ribbon. I accept the result. It's a popular contest and draws many of the nation's producers.

The same is true in January at the MMPA annual state meeting and contest, where I enter the other pint sample of dark amber syrup. I score 96 points in the MMPA contest and, again, no ribbon. Syrup density, likely measured by the same refractometer used at Bar Harbor, is 66.3° Brix, 0.7° below the Bar Harbor reading of 67.0°. The Maple Syrup Producers Manual published by NAMSC says the accuracy and readability of hand-held refractometers is within approximately 0.2° Brix. Go figure. I can insert my Colonel Ayres hydrotherm into a test cup of syrup one hundred consecutive times and obtain the same reading every time.

Irrespective of the discourse over use of the Ayres Hydrotherm, however, I enter two different samples in the MMPA's 2011 contest at the Maine Agricultural Show: medium amber and dark amber. The dark amber, 66.8° Brix, scores 95 points and earns a white ribbon for third place. The medium amber, 67.0° Brix, scores a perfect 100 points, earns the blue ribbon in its class and Best of Show overall, warranting a picture-taking session and our name, Jackson Mountain Farm, engraved on the Orlando & Gertrude Small Memorial trophy. "This will look just great displayed in the saphouse on Maine Maple Sunday," Beth declares.

I continue a participant in the syrup contest a few more years. But tasting becomes faddish with the judges, and my syrup is continually judged buddy, or woody, or smoky, or burnt, or some otherwise recently discovered fashionable off-flavor. So I drop out of contests and focus on my customers for verification of my syrup's quality. They love the taste of it—and they tell me so.

Chapter Twenty-Three

MAINE MAPLE SUNDAY

THE PRINCIPAL MISSION OF THE MAINE MAPLE PRODUCERS ASSOCIA-
tion, according to its bylaws, is to "promote Pure Maine Maple Syrup and
its subsequent products." Since 1946 when the MMPA came into being,
its board has focused mainly on promoting the products of its producers:
syrup, sugar, candy, creams, and butters at festivals, fairs, meetings, open
houses, and public events. The association lectures, advertises, publicizes,
displays, sells, and donates maple syrup on behalf of Maine's producers.
The MMPA exists for that purpose. Thus, the formation of the MMPA
may have been the most important event in Maine sugaring history. It
brought sugarmakers together for a common purpose.

The Maine Maple Festival and Sugaring-off Party in Strong was
one of the MMPA's first attempts at public promotion of Maine maple
syrup. First held in 1959, the festival, sponsored jointly by the Strong
Lions Club, the Maine Maple Producers Association, and the Maine
Department of Agriculture, featured a Saturday celebration in April, sort
of a commemoration and celebration of the recent season, a sugaring-off
party featuring a parade, demonstrations, syrup on ice cream, a best maple
syrup contest, a pancake banquet, the naming of a Maine Maple Queen,
and a ball with live music, a something-for-everyone party. Hundreds of
people made the journey to Strong for the annual day-long celebration.
The festival lasted maybe seven years. In 1968 it was gone.

The Maine Maple Syrup Association was not discouraged by the
disappearance of the Strong festival. The setback more likely prompted
the association to strike out in a new direction. MMPA reacted by simply

moving its boastful maple syrup promotions to someone else's festival. It replaced the Maine Maple Festival and Sugaring-off Party with a plethora of promotions and demonstrations, all at other festive Maine celebrations. It constructed prototype saphouses at Maine's Agricultural Fairs—Fryeburg, Cumberland, Farmington, and Skowhegan—where MMPA hyped and sold pure Maine maple syrup. It erected a promotional booth at the La Kermesse Franco-Americaine Festival in Biddeford, built a saphouse on wheels, and promoted Maine maple syrup at the Sugarloaf Ski Association's sugaring-off party at Carrabassett Valley in April, and staffed a shopping kiosk during a holiday weekend at the Maine Mall in South Portland, where holiday shoppers could buy just the right gift.

In 2011, MMPA created Maple Mania, a summer weekend of sociability that included a saphouse tour, a technical learning session, and vendors' exhibits. Sugarmakers, equipment manufacturers, and researchers—perhaps as many as two hundred—came to Maine's Maple Mania from the maple-producing states and provinces and set off a flood of publicity for "Maine maple syrup and its subsequent products." Guests visited as many as ten sugaring sites during a tour into Maine's hills, questioned lecturers on a myriad of contemporary sugaring issues at the technical sessions, and frequently tasted Maine's official sweetener, maple syrup, along the way.

These promotions—fairs, festivals, and Maple Mania—have come into being since the ending of Strong's sugaring-off party in 1968. For the most part, they are still in place—and doing well. But the blockbuster creation of all MMPA promotions is Maine Maple Sunday™, a statewide saphouse open house celebrating Maine sugaring.

In 2002, Jackson Mountain Farm officially hosts Maine Maple Sunday for the first time. It's the twentieth such statewide open house since 1983. Though I, as a member of the MMPA board, participated in its founding, perhaps even suggested it be called Maine Maple Sunday, I have not celebrated it with a formal, advertised open house during the twenty years of its existence. The twenty years have been working years for Beth and me. And we didn't find the time for extras, particularly the wherewithal to pull off such an annual gala as a Maine Maple Sunday celebration. Though our saphouse door was always open, and folks in town knew they were welcome to come and watch whatever's happening inside, preparing for Maine Maple Sunday was out of the question—until our retirement from the workaday world in 2000. Come 2002, we choose to host an open house on Maine Maple Sunday and show off what we do on Orchard Hill.

On the fourth Sunday in March, Beth gathers up ice cream and popcorn and coffee and chocolate powder and drinking water, I leave directions on the answering machine for any last-minute queries, and we go to the saphouse. Grass is visible in Temple's fields for the first time since mid-November. It's a welcome sight to us, and likely also to a lonely robin in Blodgett's field that a week ago flitted around on two feet of snow.

At 11:00 a.m. we officially—and literally—open our door. Before noon the first guests arrive, a young mother and daughter who live around the corner on Varnum Pond Road. The daughter has waited for weeks, her mother says, to see the inside of our saphouse and where the steam comes from. Mother lifts daughter high enough to look into the boiling pans. Daughter pulls mother down to taste the syrup, eat popcorn, and drink hot chocolate. More folks come through the door. They come single and in groups, drink in the steam, and ask the obligatory question between sips of coffee, or hot chocolate, "How many gallons of sap does it take, anyways, to make a gallon of syrup?"

Over the next ninety minutes, I smile and chat, and answer questions while drawing off about three gallons of syrup from the boiling pan. Beth, with the help of a friend who drove three miles here from Walker's Hill through axle-deep mud to reach our sugar shack, filters the new syrup, reheats it, and bottles it in glass and plastic jugs suitable for the kitchen table.

Jack and Bill are here to help us celebrate. Bill metes out our meager supply of syrup for sale and tends to the cash box. Jack, here from Boston with Victoria and the grandkids, taps six sugar maples trees along the road in front of the saphouse, while the grandkids watch. "So folks driving by will know what's going on here," he says. But most whom come to our first official open house—something more than fifty and less than a thousand—stay around until I shut down the evaporator.

One person, a somewhat curious professor from the University of Maine at Farmington whose name I didn't get, paces the saphouse floor, peeks into obscure nooks here and there, asks small questions, and sips syrup from a sample cup. At about three o'clock, our advertised closing time, he looks at me and says, "This is the best tasting syrup I've had."

"Have you tasted anyone else's?" I query.

"Yes I have," he answers, "I've tasted three others today." I glance at the person with him, a shorter, stouter man who looks more experienced in maple tasting. He nods in agreement.

Maine Maple Sunday was constructively born at the 1982 MMPA annual meeting when the membership elected Arnold Luce, an Anson producer, president of the association. Son or grandson of three former Maine maple producers, Luce headed Luce's Maple Syrup in Anson, the fourth generation in his family during a period of one hundred years to sugar on the same site. A forward-thinking progressive, he took over an ancestry farm of 1,700 tapholes and a four-foot-by-twelve-foot oil-fired Leader Special evaporator. He converted his father's sap-gathering system from buckets to plastic tubing, and in 1984, his tap count nearing 3,500, he took the plunge into reverse osmosis, first in Maine to do so. Though reverse osmosis was expensive to install and he needed to modify his saphouse to keep the membranes from freezing, he made it work, finding improved efficiencies and higher profits in a lesser number of boiling hours per day. He had caught, as so many others had at that time, maple fever.

Luce's ambitious switched to tubing, and the expansion of his bush resulted in dramatic improvements in sap yield and boiling efficiencies. His boiling rig—including the 1984 reverse osmosis—could process considerably more sap than in the preexpansion days of the 1960s and

1970s, fully as much as his sugarbush would yield. His rig produced twice the number of gallons per hour his father and grandfathers had produced out of the same set of pans, putting him in position to improve his gross profit. But only if he could generate similar improvements in the marketplace.

As president of the Maine Maple Producers Association, Luce applied the same forward thinking he used in his own sugarbush. His interests, however, had turned to marketing, and his terms—he served two, two-year terms as president of the MMPA—emphasized the principal tenet of the MMPA mission, promotion of maple syrup and maple products. Ted Greene, a Sebago producer—seventh generation—and secretary of MMPA during Luce's time as president, recalls Board of Director meetings when nearly all of the discussion centered on the promotion and marketing of Maine-made maple syrup. It was requisite as president, Luce believed, that he work on behalf of the membership.

At the MMPA Board of Directors meeting at Skowhegan in February 1983, Secretary Greene noted in his minutes such a discussion. Talk focused on how the MMPA could best and foremost assist all Maine producers with promotion of their syrup and syrup products. Luce led the discussion. Directors present included Greene; Bob Smith, a Skowhegan producer who tapped a roadside bush in several southern Somerset County towns and boiled off syrup in downtown Skowhegan; Chester Basford, a former spout and bucket producer from Benton Station, Maine, who advocated the use of plastic tubing; John Steeves, a forty-year veteran of sugaring in Skowhegan who saw no limits on sugaring's future; Peter Tracy, a producer whose Maple Hill Farm in Farmington is the descendant farm of Maine maple syrup originator Stephen Titcomb; and others, including myself from Jackson Mountain Farm in Temple. What resulted from the Luce-led discussion was the launching of a signature Maine event—a statewide open saphouse Sunday—that would eventually reverberate all across the maple world. Termed Maine Maple Sunday by Ted Greene—some think the term came from me, but I don't recall exercising such innovative thinking then—the event would feature a statewide open saphouse regale annually on the fourth Sunday in March, a celebration to recognize and promote Maine's long-standing maple syrup heritage. The board voted unanimously to go ahead immediately.

The first Maine Maple Sunday took place barely six weeks later, March 27, 1983. It was a first-in-the-nation event. A dozen Maine producers hosted open houses. "Come and see Maine maple syrup made," they broadcast. Entertainment featured syrup making, sleigh rides, sap-collecting tours, syrup tasting, pancake breakfasts, maple sundaes, and syrup selling. Acceptance by the public was unexpectedly high. Maple Hill Farm in Farmington counted 1,500 visitors. Jillson Farm in Litchfield sold out of maple syrup and, before the day had ended, out of the fruits and vegetables preserved in their farmhouse cellar as well. And the event would grow. Two years later in 1985, benefiting from the considerable assistance of Sherry Moen, marketing specialist at the Maine Department of Agriculture, nineteen saphouses hosted Maine Maple Sunday open houses, and producers recorded twelve thousand visits.

Soon Maine Maple Sunday had become so popular that similar celebrations sprung up all across the northeastern and midwestern United States from New Hampshire to Ohio and beyond. Many of the other thirteen maple-producing states had adopted Maine's lead, affixing such names to competing events as Maple Syrup Weekend, Open House Weekend, All-Things-Maple Month, Maple Festival, and Maple Madness. Consequently, MMPA, to protect Maine's unique descriptor from being duplicated by others, registered its trademark name, Maine Maple Sunday™.

The media, too, found Maine Maple Sunday a source of popular news. Through effective media promotion and local advertising, the Maine Maple Producers Association and its partner, the Maine Department of Agriculture, promoted producer participation in the annual celebration year after year—and more and more folks discovered the maple syrup–making gala and came out and celebrated. In 2013, the thirtieth anniversary of Maine Maple Sunday™, participation by producers and the public reached new highs: more than one hundred participating open saphouses and more than fifty thousand visitors, all despite a March spell of midsummer weather that forced many producers to preserve previous sap runs and boil them off on Maine Maple Sunday, so their guests could "come and see Maine maple syrup made."

Jackson Mountain Farm follows its 2002 debut with continuing participation. Though we are located a bit too far north for reliable sugaring weather on the inflexible fourth Sunday in March, we improvise: we show *Life on Jackson Mountain*, the video Bill Hodgkins put together some years ago; we serve hot drinks; we offer maple-flavored snacks and a bit of syrup to taste; we explain the process and conduct short walking tours; and usually, regardless of the weather—or the temperature—we host a goodly number of people. Customarily, we boil what sap we have about midday and spend the remainder of the four hours entertaining guests and selling the syrup we've made thus far. In the case of bad weather, or only a bit of sap, we save the previous day's sap run for the boil. With no sap, however, we might light the fire and push the almost-syrup in the pans with water to illustrate how the rig works. Often we have syrup to filter, which gathers a small crowd around the press. Or we may have something special to mark the day, Beth's acclaimed maple syrup squares, for example, or more.

At the 2011 Maine Maple Sunday, of course, we advertise our "Best of Show" trophy, which brings folks in to see the making of Maine's best maple syrup. In 2013 we celebrate the thirtieth anniversary of Maine Maple Sunday and display a plaque recognizing Jackson Mountain Farm as one of the contributing founders. And in 2014 we celebrate our fiftieth anniversary of syrup making, which encourages a record crowd on Orchard Hill Road. We mark the occasion with a small memento, a 30 ml glass bottle of Jackson Mountain Farm's notable light amber syrup in the shape of a maple leaf.

Folks like our syrup, and say so. "Best I've tasted," one says. "Looking forward to another season of your famous maple syrup," another chimes. "We'd love some more of your amazing maple syrup" and "This syrup is the best I've ever tasted" are typical comments we hear in the saphouse on Maine Maple Sunday. And I tell them, we're one of the few saphouses nowadays where you can actually see the sap boil.

Maine Maple Sunday is good for Maine maple producers. It brings publicity and customers and cash to saphouses all over Maine. Also compliments. I suspect former association president Arnold Luce, who first suggested Maine producers set aside a Sunday for the public to learn of our existence and come out to see what we do, and who is now busy with his own Maine Maple Sunday open saphouse in Anson, is pleased, as well, that some years ago now the MMPA board gave unanimous consent to his recommendation.

CHAPTER TWENTY-FOUR

MAINE MAPLE BEYOND PANCAKES

IN 2005, BETH HODGKINS PROPOSES TO THE MMPA BOARD OF DIREC-
tors that MMPA publish a recipe book citing the many ways maple syrup
can be used in the kitchen. She is inspired by WCSH-TV weatherman
Kevin Mannix, whom she caught suggesting to his viewers that they stay
indoors during a pending snowstorm and enjoy some "good old-fashioned
Vermont maple syrup on a plate of pancakes."

"I'm tired of hearing people promote Vermont's maple syrup," she
appeals to the board. "Don't they know we make maple syrup here in
Maine?" Beth suggests she lead a small committee that will somehow
compile a number of recipes that use, or could use, maple syrup as an
ingredient. These recipes would be joined with stories, personal stories
that would illumine pure Maine maple syrup, and perhaps enlighten the
readers as well. The book would also include useful information: how
syrup is made and graded, for example, and how to buy it, whether from
a store or a producer.

She also recommends that MMPA publish and distribute the recipe
book to sugarmakers, bookstores, and the general public. And she predicts the book will be popular in Maine kitchens, perhaps sell as many
as two thousand copies. A similar cookbook, she adds, the Maine wild
blueberry grower's version, sells at L.L. Bean in Freeport and claims
"more than 50,000 copies sold."

Discussion of her proposal is mainly favorable, but the board is
not unanimous. Al Bolduc objects. "Can't make any money with it," he
says. Someone reminds Bolduc of the association's mission: promotion

of maple syrup and its subsequent products. What better way is there, someone else asks, to publicize Maine's maple industry than with a book describing more than a hundred different uses of maple syrup in the kitchen? More discussion takes place. Bolduc is persuaded. The board's vote is unanimous. Beth and her meager cookbook committee are in the book-writing business.

Her first step is a search for recipes. She solicits them directly: by telephone, email, and post. She writes to every Maine producer, including French-speaking Quebeckers in Somerset County, and asks them to contribute a favorite maple syrup recipe—with a story. She also contributes stories and memories of her own maple syrup childhood into the pages, and relates tales of her first experiences at Jackson Mountain Farm. She adds advice and maple savvy: how to speak maple syrup, how to buy it, how to store it. She forwards the French submissions from Quebec to Patricia Hodgkins, a retired French teacher in Salem, New Hampshire, for interpretation. And asks Pat Jillson and Penny Savage, themselves Maine maple syrup producers, to read it critically. She entreats Val Vaughan, a former newspaper contributor, to edit portions; persuades husband John to produce a cover; solicits Earle Mitchell, a Bowdoin producer, to sketch illustrations; hires Ginny Raye, a book designer in Pittsfield, to design it; and contracts with Ink Blot Printing in Vassalboro to print it. In 2007 she turns the finished product over to the publisher, MMPA. Price tag: $10.95.

Maine Maple beyond Pancakes is an instant hit. It is sold in bookstores in Farmington, Norway, Augusta, and the Village Store in Shin Pond, Maine. Every sugar shack in Maine displays it for sale on Maine Maple Sunday. At Jackson Mountain Farm, Beth brings a signing pen to our Maine Maple Sunday open house, and every book sold is autographed by the author. She is asked to host a book talk in Farmington, and later is the guest speaker at the Fortnightly Club, a one-hundred-year-old Yarmouth ladies club, where she reads and autographs for the members. Sales of autographed copies are also brisk in Beth's kitchen. Eight years later MMPA has sold six thousand copies, not a record-breaking number, but enough to warrant acknowledgement that *Maine Maple beyond Pancakes* is a promotional success.

Chapter Twenty-Five

GRADING MAPLE SYRUP

GRADING MAPLE SYRUP IS NOT COMPLICATED. IN 2010 JACKSON MOUNtain Farm grades its maple syrup the same as everyone else. I put a sample jar of syrup in a color comparator and hold it up to a light, the sun, the sky, a light bulb, and pick where it fits in the hierarchy of colors: light amber, medium amber, dark amber, or, since 1993 when the Maine Legislature approved a fourth grade, extra dark amber. The color of maple syrup, its grade, is determined every day—every batch—in a somewhat crude comparator according to its aptitude to transmit light. Continual grading is necessary because the sap loses sugar as the season progresses, requiring more boiling to reach standard density syrup. The longer boiling time darkens the syrup a bit. So we grade every batch.

The taste of syrup also changes as the season lengthens. The lighter syrup, which normally comes first, has a somewhat delicate maple taste, and the darker grades—medium, dark, and extra dark—taste progressively stronger. The slight change in taste, I have observed, occurs at about the point where the grade changes from one color to another. It is a distinct change, common to the experienced taste buds. Maple syrup loses its delicate taste, for example, when it loses its light amber designation. The medium amber takes on a bit heavier flavor, as well, also noticeable to the experienced taste buds. The dark amber, in turn, assumes a richer and stronger taste, and so on down the scale to Maine's extra dark amber, which is the strongest of all. Beyond that point, Maine's maple syrup may approach bitter or buddy, and is graded commercial.

That tasters can perceive a taste change at the point of a grade change is no accident. It is taste, I suspect, that controls the range of color grades we use today. Before the onset of color comparators, say before the twentieth century, producers tasted their syrup and perhaps dropped a dite of it on a flat piece of tin and observed it before calling out its grade. If it didn't look light and taste light, it wasn't light. If it didn't look dark and taste dark, it wasn't dark. For consistency, producers likely—and logically—developed color comparators to indicate what they had learned from their experience. And that's how it is. The categories of maple syrup are defined by the syrup's taste. Syrup that tastes good is pancake good, syrup that doesn't taste good isn't, a truth in the Maine maple syrup industry since the time of Stephen Titcomb in 1781. But now comes the International Maple Syrup Institute.

The International Maple Syrup Institute is an association of associations. Nine states, four provinces, and innumerable producers, manufacturers, and individuals comprise the institute. It started in 1974 when Dr. L. David Garrett, director of the USDA Maple Research Laboratory, presiding over a discussion of depressed market conditions with representatives of the maple syrup industry, suggested that "an international organization of processors, producers, and government representatives be formed to work out an international marketing strategy." In February 1975, seventy members of American and Canadian maple product industries met in Plattsburg, New York, and agreed to bylaws creating the International Maple Syrup Institute. Eighteen members of the North American maple industry, the founders, affixed their names to the bylaws formally establishing IMSI.

The institute, whose mission is to promote and protect pure maple products worldwide, customarily deals with market-related challenges. Such matters as international surpluses and shortages of syrup, the health of the tree, pest control, and other troubles that may jeopardize the industry or its resources, commonly appear on the institute's agenda. The IMSI meets twice each year, jointly with the North American Maple Syrup Council.

About 2002, IMSI formed a committee of its members to, the institute announced, determine a way to make the industry's grading system less cumbersome to consumers and packers. Several iterations of grading nomenclature were then in place in the states and provinces, allegedly causing difficulty for consumers to know what they were buying; for example, the difference between light and fancy syrup or even light and dark. Packers also, if buying syrup from another jurisdiction, were having trouble describing what they wanted; for example, dark amber, or grade B. The committee worked at the issue for three years and then in October 2004 submitted a report at a Lake George, New York, meeting of IMSI.

The committee's report acknowledged the difficulties with geographic grading systems and recommended that a standardized grading system reaching across all maple-producing states and provinces be implemented. A draft proposal was accepted by both the IMSI and NAMSC boards of directors, stating that changes needed to occur in the law and in the descriptors—color and taste—of the various grades, but changes in the basic grading structure were not necessary. Maple syrup would be described in words that depicted its looks and its taste; for example, golden delicate or dark robust. Color boundaries would not change. The committee, the Standardized Maple Grades and Nomenclature Committee, headed by David Chapeskie of Ontario, would continue to define the international standards for classifying maple syrup.

In late summer 2008, following Chapeskie's appointment by the IMSI Board of Directors to executive director, IMSI engaged a research firm, Cintech Agroalimentaire, to determine consumer preferences for color, flavor, and origin of maple syrup, and to come up with a descriptive term for each grade that best expressed what appealed to consumers. In August 2009 at an IMSI board meeting in Fredericton, New Brunswick, the consultant submitted a standard grades and classification proposal for the international industry to consider.

At the Fredericton meeting, recommendations for syrup grading changes appeared in the proposal for the first time. IMSI's Board of Directors ignored the recommended changes, however, and unanimously accepted as the preferred classification system three classes of grade A syrup suitable for sale in retail markets, and one class of grade B syrup for food processing and flavoring. This proposal, similar to the grading currently in place in Maine, involved combining various light amber classes of syrup in current use internationally—Fancy, light, A, and AA—into a single light class and leaving the darker classes of grade A syrup with only minor adjustments. Grade B would comprise all syrup unsuitable as grade A. The approved proposal was to be reviewed by IMSI members and would be put on the agenda for discussion and vote at the board meeting in October at Bar Harbor, Maine.

Lyle Merrifield, vice president of the Maine Maple Producers Association, and Kathy Hopkins, professor and maple products specialist at the University of Maine Cooperative Extension, serve on the IMSI Board of Directors. Professor Hopkins is Maine's maple specialist and educator, and has a history of hard work on behalf of the Maine Maple Producers Association. She has been editor of *Maple News*, the MMPA's quarterly newsletter, for many years. She conducts educational seminars and training sessions open to producers in Maine, New Hampshire, and Vermont on procedures for making high-quality maple syrup; for example, recognizing and eliminating off-taste syrup and developing effective and sanitary syrup-processing procedures. She is the author of Maine's *Maple Syrup Quality Control Manual* published by the University of Maine Cooperative Extension, an important and successful publication of best practices from taphole cleanliness to filling containers. Hopkins deserves much credit for the progress made by Maine producers toward high-quality maple syrup. She manages syrup contests at the MMPA annual meeting, at the Maine summer gala Maple Mania, and at the NAMSC annual meeting when it's in Maine. She has lectured and spoken and taught and wheedled for the past several years supporting IMSI's move toward standardized maple grades. She is well versed in the work required to make good syrup and, I suspect, a very effective and persuasive voice on the IMSI Board of Directors.

Lyle Merrifield is currently vice president of the Maine Maple Producers Association. Elected in 2009, Merrifield, a small producer in Gorham and former president of the Southern Maine Maple Sugarmakers

Association (SMMSA)—now a subchapter of MMPA—is new to the IMSI board. He is one of the founders of the SMMSA and, during his service there, an active member of MMPA, serving on its board prior to being elected vice president in 2009. Merrifield is maple savvy and brings a neutral voice to the IMSI board.

At the 2009 Annual Meeting in Bar Harbor, the IMSI Board of Directors, Hopkins and Merrifield in support, endorse the final version of the standardization proposal, which comprises a surprising transition to new maple syrup grades—new grades were ruled out in the originally approved 2004 proposal—and adoption of new maple syrup descriptors, all to be implemented over a multiyear period but not before 2013. This change in grading expands the number and breadth of maple syrup grades suitable for sale in retail markets from three to four and includes the entire light transmittance band from 100 percent Tc to zero Tc, enabling consumer grade syrup to be sold for table-top use with 0 percent light transmittance. The proposal divides the spectrum of light transmittance into equal quarters, each quarter a different grade and presumably a different taste. Color and taste descriptors will be determined by Cintech Agroalimentaire and its three hundred research tasters, one hundred of which reside in New Jersey.

Such a significant change in maple syrup grading is controversial in Maine. At the MMPA annual meeting a few producers resist the change, citing the obvious tendency toward including darker syrups under the grade A label and relying on taste-based grading by the producers. Using such syrups as pancake-grade toppings, they say, will weaken the perceived quality of Maine maple syrup in the marketplace. But more producers, citing the growing popularity of darker syrup, embrace the change, saying that the demand for darker syrup warrants producing more of it—and at a premium price. This discussion, however, does not move the MMPA Board of Directors to act.

Instead, MMPA invites Executive Director David Chapeskie, of the International Maple Syrup Institute and chair of the IMSI's Maple Grades Committee, to Maine. He comes to our 2012 Annual Meeting at the Augusta Civic Center and presents the IMSI's proposed standardized maple syrup grading system to the membership. MMPA allocates two hours at the lectern for Chapeskie. But he doesn't come to conduct a hearing or moderate a vote. He comes to solicit acceptance from Maine producers. He comes to persuade Maine producers to adopt the new grading standards—or not.

Maine producers know, however, as does MMPA officialdom, that many of their customers prefer the darker side of the current grading system. Maine's dark amber and extra dark amber syrup "tastes like real maple syrup," some customers are heard to say, unlike years ago when light—or Fancy—grade maple syrup was held up as the quintessence of suburban pancake toppings, and more than a few producers put a premium price on it because of its eminence. But the taste of popular syrup has trended toward the darker side in recent years. MMPA's sampling stations at fair booths and trade shows have recorded a new preference for medium amber and dark amber syrups. The Cintech Agroalimentaire and their New Jersey tasters verify what Maine syrup producers already know. Maine producers have been receiving numerous requests for dark syrup for many years; "I'd prefer dark syrup if you have it," we hear. Back in the early 1990s, Maine producers made their own move to expand the availability of darker maple syrup.

In 1992 the Board of Directors at MMPA, aware even then that more of the spectrum could be sold as tabletop retail syrup, voted to convert a portion of the darker commercial grade to an extra dark retail grade. At that time Maine syrup with less than 44 percent Tc was being marketed as grade B commercial and sold to industrial producers of maple-flavored food and tobacco products. Yet frequently a retail customer would request specifically a quart or half-gallon of grade B commercial to use in cooking. A few producers made a bit of grade B commercial specifically for that purpose. So MMPA felt comfortable that the lighter zone of grade B commercial syrup, properly filtered and graded and tasted, would be suitable for the retail market and submitted a proposal to the Maine legislature to add a fourth grade. East Sebago producer Ted Greene, president of MMPA then, testified at the public hearing accompanied by producers Bob Smith and John Hodgkins.

Greene, who produced maple syrup at Macs Corner in East Sebago, was the quintessential maple producer. His grandfather Arthur, a farmer and logger, had first made syrup on the Mac's Corner rocky hillsides in 1914, a flat pan on a stone arch. Greene and his family have continued the family tradition. In the 1960s Greene demonstrated his progressiveness by putting in about five hundred tapholes on Maple Flo plastic tubing, tubing that he continues to use in 1992. At the hearing, he presented detailed information to the legislature's Agricultural Committee pertaining to grading maple syrup.

Greene's testimony to the committee—Smith's and Hodgkins's, as well—was persuasive. The committee agreed that Maine needed a fourth grade, that customers were desirous of a stronger, darker syrup to use in cooking and baking and as a topping on pancakes and waffles, and that a goodly amount of the currently commercial grade B—that between 44 percent Tc and 27 percent Tc—was suitable for tabletop use. Below 27 Tc, syrup would remain grade B commercial. The legislature's Agricultural Committee approved the extra dark amber proposal unanimously without further discussion, effective in the 1993 season. When Chapeskie arrived at the Augusta Civic Center in 2012 to sell his proposal, Maine producers had been marketing grade A extra dark amber maple syrup for nearly ten years. MMPA didn't need his grading scheme. Some felt he needed ours.

Reaction to Chapeskie's presentation at the Augusta Civic Center is mixed. The officers are by and large in favor of it and will likely support anything Chapeskie proposes. The members, however, seem generally disinterested. One expresses concern that the IMSI has gone too far in expanding tabletop grade syrup into the low light zone, that extra dark maple syrup, now being hyped as table grade syrup, is actually the residue of the maple syrup season; the syrup that producers commonly truck off to processors as grade B commercial syrup, unfit for the kitchen table. Chapeskie's proposal will allow it to be poured onto pancakes and vanilla ice cream.

A second also argues that the IMSI proposal goes too far, that producers will be selling the bottom of the color classes, the lees, so to speak, less than 27 percent Tc, for use on waffles and biscuits. Maine will "become just another piece of a worldwide product, its identity lost in the paperwork."

No MMPA member speaks in support of Chapeskie's proposal.

The MMPA Board of Directors fails to respond to ISMI's proposal. Led by President Lyle Merrifield and Professor Kathy Hopkins, who sit on the IMSI board, and for reasons of simplicity and logic in the worldwide scheme of maple syrup production, Maine passes on protecting their iconic identity and quietly accepts the IMSI decree. Labels will be ready in 2013, mandatory in 2015.

At Jackson Mountain Farm in 2012, however, we have little to do with syrup or syrup dealers or packers outside Maine's borders. The IMSI standardized grading causes us no concern, nor should it. I am aware that the grading change is designed to benefit not just producers and retailers, but also the entire maple syrup world: producers, packers, retailers, consumers, and buyers and sellers in the marketplace. Consumers looking for high-grade Maine maple syrup in 2015 when the new labeling becomes mandatory will find it on Orchard Hill Road in Temple, as they have for years. They will also find in all the grades save light amber a somewhat darker and stronger tasting syrup, and thereby, our taste polling tells us, a richer tasting syrup.

Taste of pure maple syrup is subjective. Taste doesn't wear a name tag. Taste has no dimensions, is not defined by length or weight or time. Its character is perceived, rather than actual or independent. Its sense is idiosyncratic—personal—to a particular individual. Though contest judges are trained—or self-trained—to pick out subtle off-flavors in maple syrup, producers are not. Not every producer can identify the nuances of taste. And I suspect judges, and perhaps in some cases consumers, have the same difficulty.

The flavor of maple syrup varies slightly from locale to locale, sugarbush to sugarbush, season to season. The flavor of maple syrup is not intended to be consistent or predictable. It is intended to be what soil, groundwater, and pure sap from the sugar maple will produce without interference of contaminate. From year to year and hillside to hillside, minor variations in flavor come naturally from the cycle of nature. This is the way of things. These things do not change. We take what is given. But the manageable characteristics of the boiling process—boiling time, cleanliness, and exposure to contaminate—can also affect flavor, and these things do require the attention of the producer.

Quick boiling of clean and pure natural sugar maple sap produces the best and truest flavor in maple syrup. At Jackson Mountain Farm, we boil sap shallow and fast. I grew up sugaring in the shadow of Maine producers who aimed to make light syrup, and I know how to do it. I watched them—Warren Voter, Ray Titcomb, Orlando Small—boil off syrup shallow and quick, which produced a taste and appearance I termed delectable, even delightful, something that would sparkle when poured over a pancake or a dish of vanilla ice cream. Since then I've desired to make lighter syrup, stayed away from the heavy end of the scale. I do, however, confess to keeping a short list of customers looking for cooking-type syrup, what MMPA's recipe book, *Maine Maple beyond Pancakes*, calls cooking syrup, and when the last boil-off comes and it's suitable for such, I make some of it. But I use the same rules, shallow and quick.

Chapeskie's standardized grading scheme is not contrary to my boiling rules, but it does, I believe, devalue the role of taste. Outside of the traditional color boundaries, meaning in the murky area of less than 30 percent light transmittance, a new mantra has emerged. "If the syrup tastes okay, the syrup is okay." Discourse over the new grades actually brings this self-imposed axiom to the classroom. Tasting for acceptability is the subject of seminars, the object of competitions. Tasting parties, featuring off-tasting syrup, are held in conference rooms and schoolhouses. And it's the producer, the lonely and stressed producer with sticky hands and cold feet, who has to make the subjective call. The introduction of IMSI's standardized grading proposal increases the likelihood that off-tastes will reach the consumer.

Professor Hopkins preaches taste. In an attempt to educate producers, she conducts tasting seminars, tasting competitions, and asks producers to identify from as many as seventeen samples displayed on a table: "Which are the off-taste samples and what is the contaminate in each?" Most folks don't know the answers. The list of contaminates that affect the flavor of maple syrup is lengthy. No longer is it only smoke. Smoke is hardly present in saphouses now. The list more likely contains such obnoxious and unexpected trouble as burnt niter, road salt, bleach, excessive defoamer, mold, paint, wood, burnt syrup, and other dreadful matter. It's a list of substances that producers don't taste every day. And when a foreign taste does cross a producer's palate, he's likely to misidentify it, mistake it for something else. The producer, however, is the bottom line in the murky zone. It's the producer who tastes it and puts the label on the package.

In 2012 I'm trying to learn. I'm trying to understand what off-flavored syrup is, how to identify the contaminate and how to prevent it from tainting my syrup. During my journey, I've tasted three samples of what is professed to be buddy syrup. Each one tastes different from the other two. I have tasted syrup made from 2 percent sap boiled for fifteen minutes and syrup made from 20 percent sap—a product of reverse osmosis—boiled perhaps less than a minute. They don't taste the same. For three consecutive years, I've submitted samples of my syrup to MMPA's annual contest. One by one, the three samples are each summarily rejected. Off-taste: buddy, woody, and burnt. Yet year after year I can't make enough of it to meet the local demand.

Professor Hopkins also lectures cleanliness as a manageable characteristic of good tasting maple syrup. Author of Maine's *Maple Syrup Quality Control Manual*, she writes that, "The most important contributor to maple syrup quality is cleanliness." She goes on to say, "Cleanliness must be obtained without using cleaning compounds, sanitizers, soaps, or bleaches." Cleaning compounds are on her list of contaminates. It's not, however, about cleaning compounds. It's about taste. Soap tastes like soap; bleach tastes like bleach. Taste lingers. The taste of maple syrup must be protected. Taste is our trademark. So what does Hopkins suggest producers use to clean dirty and sticky tools and countertops? "Plenty of elbow grease and lots of clean, hot water," she writes.

Grading maple syrup may be uncomplicated, but it's sure not easy.

THE REVOLUTION

IT'S 2011 ON ORCHARD HILL ROAD. JACKSON MOUNTAIN FARM'S CON-version to a contemporary gathering system is complete, high tech, up to date, modern—again. We have completed the transition to check-valve spouts and added sap ladders in low places where sap needs to be lifted up to gain the storage tank. We are using reliable vacuum—16 inHg—to discourage bacteria from migrating to tapholes. We have no visible or audible vacuum leaks. Sap runs into the evenings until the temperature is well below freezing. The check valves do their job and bacteria aren't visibly affecting the sap flow, which holds at a midseason level for the duration of the season. And we produce 143 gallons of maple syrup, enough to convince us that our gathering system is behaving.

Eric Ellis, president of the Maine Maple Producers Association, comes by Orchard Hill Road after the season ends in April and invites me to participate in MMPA's first Maple Mania, a three-day showcase of Maine's maple syrup technologies being held at the University of Maine Farmington in June. "We're inviting all the producing states and provinces to come and see what we have here," he tells me. "We'd like to include your saphouse on the tour, show off the sap ladders."

"I'd love to!" I answer, though I know I don't have facilities for the guests, adequate parking, or hardly a place for a bus to get off the road, or even turn around. "I'll be ready," I tell Ellis, and by the time June comes we've cleaned up the grounds, polished and assembled the Leader Special, and rented a facility.

They come in two buses, one at a time. Joe and Beth tend to the snacks and items for sale. I prop open the saphouse doors and feed water into a nearby sap ladder, one of our five home-fashioned devices that, under vacuum, lift sap up to where it can flow into our elevated storage tank. The guests gather where they can see into the saphouse and up the hill beyond into the sugarbush. I stand on a self-made step stool and tell them what they're looking at, describe the "high-tech, up-to-date, modern sap processing system" that we claim to have here.

"We put in seven hundred twenty-five taps on this hillside," I say. "Sap is gathered by vacuum, about 16 inHg, via a network of plastic tubing that runs directly into a five-hundred-gallon storage tank at the saphouse. Five sap ladders in the tubing network eliminate all manual sap collection and pumping. In one instance sap is lifted from a low place in the sugarbush some twenty-one feet in three lifts before it reaches the tank."

"Sap here varies from 2 percent sugar to 2.2 percent. It is boiled in a three-foot-by-twelve-foot Leader Special open-pan evaporator sitting on a home-fashioned concrete block arch that's fired by nine gallons of fuel oil per hour and produces two and one-half gallons of syrup in the hour. Annual syrup production has increased about 80 percent since converting to check-valve spout adapters, reaching 143 gallons—about one and one-half pints per taphole—this year."

"Finished syrup is filtered through a five-inch, hand-pumped press, reheated to one hundred ninety degrees Fahrenheit and packed in glass and plastic ready for sale. Sales are mainly retail to consumers. Starting in early February, we build a list of orders received from an e-mail solicitation of previous customers and other direct contacts. As syrup is produced it is packed to the list, interrupted only by walk-in sales and Maine Maple Sunday."

Following the spiel, guests wander into the saphouse for coffee and maple snacks, roam the grounds into the bush, and stop a minute to chat on their way to the bus. A Pennsylvania producer comes out of the woods and tells me I have healthier trees than he sees in his state, and asks me whether I've seen the Asian longhorned beetle, a particularly destructive sugar maple pest that is threatening New England. "No," I say. Bruce Gillilan, Vermont maple producer and sales manager at Leader Evaporator Company, comes back from a walk up the hill and tells me my tubing layout is not up to date. "It could be improved some, John." I acknowledge Bruce's well-meaning comment and make a mental note. Someone asks me whether I tap any red maples. I say yes, one, and I may pull the spout on that one. Then the tour is over. A second bus comes after lunch. It's a landmark day for Jackson Mountain Farm.

In 2011, however, the breakthrough in producing maple syrup is not about Jackson Mountain Farm. Maine is in the turmoil of a sugaring revolution. In 2011, licensed Maine producers put in 1.5 million taps, the most ever, and produce 360,000 gallons of maple syrup—one quart per taphole—also a record, continuing the upsurge of Maine maple syrup production that began in the mid-1980s. New technology—plastic tubing and applied vacuum—has sparked a passion to produce more syrup. Sugaring is popular. Producers are expanding, seeking more sap and less cost per gallon to turn it into maple syrup. New producers come into the business and open new sources. Annual production of Maine maple syrup, one hundred thousand gallons in 1989, reaches two hundred thousand gallons at the beginning of the new millennium, 360,000 gallons in 2011. Producers in the large seek a fit with trending technology, look for a way to use plastic tubing and vacuum and modern gathering and evaporating systems that will produce more sap and lessen the cost of making a gallon of maple syrup. The fervor spreads statewide.

Producers find the answers in a host of new and efficient practices, technical improvements that come from the Proctor Maple Research Center, from equipment manufacturers, from trial and error, from logical reasoning, and even from, as Plato wrote, "Necessitie, the inuentour of all goodnesse." Producers apply the ideas. They rearrange their plastic networks, concentrate and preheat their sap, increase the area of hot surface in their evaporators, switch to cost-effective fuels, and shorten their boiling times. Small producers too, those with less than a thousand taps, adapt these practices to the size of their own sugarbushes and find the same benefits—more syrup, less cost.

One producer who amends his process is Russell Black at Black Acres Farm in Wilton. Black raises beef and pork, hay, honey, hardwood lumber, and maple syrup on a farm his parents established in 1963. A typical Maine small producer—started tapping thirty-five trees at age ten—he puts in a few less than a thousand taps in 2011. Boils off his syrup on an undersized three-foot-by-eight-foot Waterloo-Small wood-fired evaporator. Though he has reached his boiling capacity, he is developing additional sugarbush on his sixty-five acres. His goal is two thousand taps. His business plan includes selling the syrup out of his saphouse on the honor system. In 2011 Black hires an energy auditor and develops plans for a new saphouse and boiling rig. He needs to meet the challenge of a thousand additional tapholes.

His energy auditor recommends reverse osmosis and a steam pan—Steam-Away—on the three-by-eight Waterloo-Small. Instead, Black replaces the Waterloo-Small with a thirty-inch-by-eight-foot CDL Intens-O-Fire—wood burning—evaporator, adds a Steam-Away heat exchanger atop the flue pan, and installs reverse osmosis rated to process two hundred gallons of sap per hour. He puts up an efficient network of plastic tubing, enough for five hundred additional tapholes, installs a small vacuum pump, and starts developing another piece of forest for five hundred more tapholes, which will give him his two thousand. Black also adds natural vacuum—three-sixteenths-inch tubing—on his steep hillsides inaccessible to his vacuum lines, and increases his induced vacuum level at the pump. His goals are the same as most Maine sugarmakers in 2011—more syrup, less cost.

Ed Jillson in Sabattus is another producer with the same goals. The Jillsons'—Ed and Pat—built a vegetable stand in Sabattus village in 1966. Soon they added maple syrup made from the sugar maples on their own land, a nominal amount of Maine-made maple syrup that they sold from the vegetable stand. But when the 1990s came and Maine syrup sales started to grow, as Jillson tells it, "We could never produce enough syrup for the demand." Jillson then expanded to small producer status—less than a thousand taps.

Jillson Farm is a diversified family business. Ed manages the maple syrup production, thirty acres of vegetable crops, and a sawmill. Two Jillson offspring, Scott and Colleen, manage eight greenhouses, and Pat manages retail sales from the farm stand and the ice cream stand. Pat also pays the bills. In 2011 the Jillson Farm gathers sap from eight hundred roadside buckets hung in three Maine counties—Androscoggin, Kennebec, and Sagadahoc—five hundred taps on a plastic tubing network in Litchfield that requires roadside pickup, and another three hundred at the Gervais Farm in Wales, which Jillson boils for Gervais on a forty-inch-by-eight-foot drop-flue, wood-fired, Leader evaporator.

In 2011 Jillson decides to expand. He calls an energy consultant in Vermont for help. He wants to increase his syrup production at less cost. His consultant recommends reverse osmosis (RO) and a steam pan. He also suggests that Ed switch fuels—wood to fuel oil. "Wood is expensive," he tells Jillson. "The most expensive fuel around." Ed doesn't agree. He installs a small RO and a Steam-Away, enough efficiency to eventually reach his goal of two thousand tapholes, and to satisfy Pat's desire for less cost.

Producers statewide similar to the Jillsons are seeking technology that fits the "more sap, less cost" philosophy. Expanded use of the popular vacuum pump is common. Many are turning up the vacuum level to 25 inHg to obtain more sap. And they're getting it. High vacuum overcomes sap-flow deficiencies in tubing systems. Lines are not as likely to fill with sap and interfere with the flow of air, which in most cases flows through the same lines.

Producers are also turning on vacuum pumps at the beginning of the season and leaving them on. A constant vacuum at the taphole eliminates backflow of bacteria-laden sap all night and all day. And producers are revising tubing layouts, increasing mainline sizes, and reducing the number of taps on a single tubing line to less than five—some perhaps as few as three. Tubing lines run less than half-full of sap, leaving space for air to be drawn out and vacuum sustained. Sap yields double.

Producers also seek increased evaporation rates. Existing boiling rigs cannot handle the flow. A hundred gallons—or even two hundred gallons—of sap evaporation on a three-foot-by-twelve-foot Leader Special in an hour, for example, doesn't do it. Six gallons of syrup an hour is not enough. Producers turn to hotter fires, higher sugar contents, increased hot boiling surfaces, and use of waste heat from steam. Attention is focused on boiling rates, boiling efficiencies, and alternate means of increasing production out of existing rigs.

The first attempt to raise the heat in boiling pans and thereby increase the evaporation rate of sap was likely the evaporator hood. The evaporator hood was popular with Maine producers when it first came on the market, perhaps in the 1950s or 1960s. Used to capture steam coming off an evaporator and funneling it up a stack pipe, the evaporator hood—or steam hood—cleared the air, so to speak, in a foggy saphouse. And, some believed, contained the steam sufficiently over the boiling sap to increase the boiling capacity, much like covering a pot of boiling potatoes on a hot stove. Others said no, a steam hood does not produce any measureable gain in sap evaporation. Consequently, Maine producers seldom installed steam hoods for boiling efficiency—until they became a necessary piece of a sap preheater.

Beginning in about the mid-1980s, inspired by the growing abundance of sap, the increasing cost of fuel, and the creative talents of the Proctor Research Labratory, a number of items known to increase sap-boiling capacity showed up in Maine saphouses. Reverse osmosis came first, of course, and was not new. Reverse osmosis, the filtering of sap under high pressure through semipermeable membranes, was first used for desalination of sea water in 1950. But come the 1980s, or perhaps a bit earlier, RO machines were designed and built to remove as much as 80 percent of the water from maple sap, increasing the sugar content of 2 percent sap, for example, to about 10 percent with a pass through an RO membrane. The resultant concentrate, say 10 percent sugar instead of the 2 percent sugar commonly found in forested sugarbushes, was boiled off in a quarter of the time, or less, and used a quarter or less fuel. It's said that at least one unknown maple producer started using reverse osmosis to remove water from sap as early as 1946, but it was not until the 1980s, when record high sap yields forced extreme methods to boil off syrup efficiently, that reverse osmosis became popular with Maine maple producers.

Arnold Luce in Anson was the first in Maine to install reverse osmosis: 1984. Luce's RO removed three-quarters of the water in his sap, and he boiled off concentrate containing 8 percent sugar. He saved himself considerable time doing so, and reduced his fuel use by three-quarters as well. By 2011 reverse osmosis had spread statewide among a modest fraction of Maine's commercial producers. Though Luce was successful, not all producers installed reverse osmosis. For some it was costly; for others, RO was not adaptable to their process and they turned to finding a way to effectively preheat sap with steam.

The idea of preheating sap prior to its entry into the flue pan was not new, either: the warming pan on a Leader Special evaporator dates to 1905. The first preheater with acceptable and consistent results, the parallel flow preheater (PFP) first arrived in manufacturer's catalogs at about the beginning of the technology revolution in the 1980s. A web of copper pipes suspended under a tight-fitting hood carried—and heated—cold sap as it flowed through the steam to the flue pan. The PFP was claimed to increase the evaporation rate of sap about 15 percent.

A step up from the parallel flow preheater was the steam pan, or Steam-Away, a heat exchanger that sat atop the flue pan, captured heat from the steam coming off boiling sap, and used it to heat incoming cold sap. The waste steam, which flowed through a network of thin-walled pipes embedded in a heat exchanger full of incoming sap, increased the temperature of sap to near its boiling point before it dropped into the flue pan. External air was also blown into the incoming sap as it flowed through the steam pan as well. The air humidified in the sap to 100 percent sap and carried away a small portion of water, said to be enough to raise the sugar content of the sap a percentage point or so. The resultant evaporation rate—gallons of incoming sap per hour—was claimed by the manufacturer to increase by about two-thirds. And the steam, which eventually condensed to pure hot water, could be saved for washing—or sold.

The Steam-Away, or steam pan, was likely first used during the rush toward more sap, perhaps just before the new millennium. Steam pans made it possible for moderate-sized producers to keep using their existing pans and fireboxes, yet boil off the sap surge that came with expansion in the 1980s and 1990s. And they could make a gallon of maple syrup with half as much fuel and have thirty gallons of distilled hot water left over. Large producers, of course, simply added steam pans into the flow of their existing rigs as well.

Other attempts during the technology revolution to increase evaporation rates and reduce energy use included using check-valve spout adapters, a means of preventing bacteria from reaching the taphole and sealing off the sap run; using three-sixteenths-inch tubing to create a natural—or no-energy—vacuum, also preventing bacteria from sealing the walls of the taphole; and blowing air into preheaters to increase—slightly—the sugar content of incoming sap.

In the case of wood-burning arches, a forced draft system was effective. Blowing large volumes of air under the grates and forcing that air up through the burning wood created a hotter fire—additional BTUs—and increased the evaporation rate some 40 percent. Wood consumption fell 20 percent in such cases, a significant savings to wood-burning producers—more sap, less cost.

In 2012, thirty-some years after the arrival of plastic tubing and vacuum, sugarbushes exist in Maine with as many as fifty thousand tapholes. Arnold Farm Sugarhouse in Sandy Bay Township is one example. Arnold Farm pumps sap through plastic pipelines more than two miles to the saphouse, where the sap is processed into maple syrup on one boiling rig. And Arnold Farm is only one example.

The last thirty years of Maine sugaring has seen the greatest improvements in sugaring technology and syrup production in Maine's history. Since the coming of Stephen Titcomb and the old kettle—they came separately—to Farmington Falls in 1781, Maine sugaring has not known such revolutionary growth, a virtual explosion in maple syrup technology and boiling capacity. Much of the capacity to produce a half million gallons of maple syrup per year comes from improvements in evaporator design.

Manufacturers are proud of the power of their evaporators. Boiling rigs in 2012, unlike those of only a few years earlier, flaunt dynamic descriptors similar in context to those of little league baseball teams and rock bands. Jackson Mountain Farm's Leader Special, what I purchased in 1990 to replace a Leader Special I purchased in 1964, is no longer in the catalogs. Equipment catalogs now reveal the current state of the art, what can be seen in manufacturer's showrooms these days. Manufacturers display such labels for their evaporation rigs as Thunderbolts, Turbos, Revolutions, Tornados, Volcanos, Vortexes, and Infernos. Such high-powered adjectives as powerflame burners, high-efficiency fireboxes, and touchscreen control devices are tags commonly used to market what one manufacturer calls the "ultimate in evaporation technique." Leader's "incomparable MAXflue pan," their catalog avows, is a pan so efficient it requires additional piping in a Steam-Away heat exchanger to capture the superfluity of heat coming from the MAXflue's rapid and extensive evaporation. Producers in 2012 concentrate sap with multiple passes through reverse osmosis membranes to more than 20 percent sugar, and boil it down to syrup in jumbo-sized evaporation rigs that efficiently produce up to 150 gallons of syrup in an hour, using but a quart of fuel oil per gallon of syrup to do so. Only a very few of these producers have ever known the pure joy of a sleek and shiny multipan Leader Special, where an observer can actually watch the sap change color as it churns and roils through open pans. Of those very few, Miguel Ibarguen at Bowley Brook Maple in Weld is one.

Bowley Brook Maple is one of the few large maple producers in organized Maine—where the cities and towns are—to have reacted vigorously to the growing attractiveness of mega-sugaring, or sugaring year-round, and put together a major production facility. The others include Strawberry Farms in Skowhegan and Kinney Maple Syrup in Knox. Ibarguen's story, however, is a story of fervor, a story of one producer and his race for equivalence. A story of what is happening during Maine sugaring's thirty-year outbreak of meteoric growth toward the top of the sugaring charts.

Ibarguen's saphouse—actually displaced living quarters he has built for year-round use for himself and his business partner, John Graham, with an evaporator in the parlor—is located on the side of Pope Mountain in the heart of Western Maine's upland hardwood forest, a tidy drive from neighboring Temple by either of two circuitous routes. The distant view from his saphouse is of Weld's forest, predominately sugar maples; the close-up view comprises stacked firewood.

Ibarguen discovered sugaring in 1983 at age three when his grandfather took him, just a toddler then, on a tour of local saphouses on Maine Maple Sunday. He saw it all that day. He watched the sap flow, the steam rise, tasted the maple syrup, and caught the passion. John Graham, who grew up on a small family farm in Weld, also caught the passion at an early age while watching his parents boil off syrup in the backyard, syrup that later appeared on his morning cereal—or flapjacks. Unknown to either of them then, their discovery occurred at the onset of Maine's sugaring upsurge. And their obsession will consume them both throughout their youth and into adulthood, Ibarguen in his grandfather's backyard and Graham on the family farm.

In 1997, Ibarguen and Graham, college freshmen and antsy for more excitement than what's found in lecture halls, pooled their resources and acquired a new, shiny Small Brothers two-foot-by-four-foot raised flue evaporator. They set it up in an aged carriage house on Graham's farm. Come the next sugaring season, Bowley Brook Maple was born.

The Small Brothers rig lasted one season. Sized to boil off some twenty-five gallons of sap per hour, the new entrepreneurs overworked their two by four, fed it more sap than Small Brothers had designed it for. The boys deemed it too slow, too little capacity for the volume of their resource, the evaporation rate out of balance with their sap supply, things you learn at a university. Hence, they sold the two-foot-by-four-foot, and replaced it with a thirty-inch-by-fourteen-foot Leader Special, a rig with forty years' experience boiling off close to one hundred gallons of sap an hour.

The forty-year-old Leader Special worked well. But at age forty-six the flue pan sprung an outsized leak, and the partners judged that a slightly smaller but tighter rig would be a better deal, so they switched to an even older three by ten with no leaks. Confident now that their rig was reliable, the partners expanded the bush and added tapholes until they had exceeded the capacity of the three by ten. Then, in the midst of Maine's sugaring explosion—2009—they leased Hurricane Mountain, a 2,300-acre plot of sugar maples located in the northeast corner of Weld up against Maine's Mt. Blue State Park and the foothills of Western Maine's mountains.

Hurricane Mountain became their breakout operation, what would put Bowley Brook Maple into the top tier of Maine maple producers and place them on the Maine maple syrup map. Ibarguen, by then a Southern Maine Technical College graduate and excavation contractor with a degree in business, and Graham, a commercial real estate professional with a degree in Rhetoric from Bates College, cleared land, built a saphouse with living accommodations, installed a septic system, and ran an electric pole line from civilized Weld to the saphouse on the flanks of Hurricane Mountain.

The first year they installed a vacuum line, a pumping station, a network of underground sap transfer pipes that would transfer sap from the forest to the storage tank, and strung tubing up the side of Hurricane Mountain sufficient to drill five thousand tapholes. At the saphouse, they put in a modern processing rig: a wood-fired, four-by-fourteen Intens-O-Fire high-efficiency evaporator, and a two-tower reverse osmosis capable of concentrating 1,200 gallons of 2 percent sap into three hundred gallons of 8 percent concentrate in an hour. A second pass through the RO would produce 12 percent concentrate.

The reverse osmosis and Intens-O-Fire combination consumed one cord of firewood and produced twenty-five gallons of maple syrup and two hundred gallons of distilled hot water in an hour. In the 2010 season, the partners' first year on Hurricane Mountain, they produced more than a thousand gallons of pure Maine maple syrup from 4,800 tapholes.

They keep drilling tapholes. In 2012 they lease another mountain—Pope Mountain—and add another five thousand tapholes, bringing their total to ten thousand. Bowley Brook's syrup production in 2012 exceeds three thousand gallons—0.33 gallons per taphole. They reach a milestone. They celebrate.

They celebrate with saphouse jazz. They rig a stage atop a nest of forty-gallon stainless steel barrels full of pure Hurricane Mountain maple syrup and invite their friends, customers, and supporters to come and listen to the Turner Templeton duo, a musical two-man band that features five instruments in the musical style of Electric Americana. Limited to the confines of Bowley Brook's saphouse and squeezed by the presence of an outsized evaporator and an assortment of storage tanks, filter presses, and bottling tanks, Electric Americana produces a hand-clapping, foot-stomping show of rock 'n' roll, blues, country, folk, and jazz, something a tourist might hear in Nashville or Clarksdale, Mississippi. Perhaps a hundred people climb up the side of Hurricane Mountain for the event, listen, applaud, and savor the time. When it's over, Ibarguen and Graham dismantle the stage and go back to sugaring.

In 2012 Maine sugaring is still in the throes of its revolution. Until the 1980s, the time of the first Maine Maple Sunday, Maine produced eight thousand gallons of maple syrup annually. Since the 1950s Maine had been stuck at eight thousand gallons per year, plus or minus a bit, and continued to produce at that level into the 1980s. The mid-1980s, however, a time when eight thousand gallons ranked Maine ninth—or tenth—of the eleven maple syrup–producing states, marked just the beginning of what would turn out to be a thirty-year revolution in sugaring technology in Maine. In 1989, Maine sugarmakers produced one hundred gallons of pure maple syrup. Ten years later Maine produced 250,000 gallons. At the time of Ibarguen's jazz fest, 2012, Maine had caught up with New York, the second largest producer of the then thirteen reporting states, at 360,000 gallons. This upsurge, upheaval, revolution really, in syrup production in Maine came from efficient sap gathering—plastic tubing and applied vacuum—and the subsequent application of new boiling technology. Maine had arrived in the sugaring world.

SOMERSET COUNTY

It's 2013. The Maine sugaring revolution goes on. Maple syrup production is up again, up to 560,000 gallons. The number of licensed producers is also up. About 450 sugarmakers, according to the Maine Department of Agriculture, are licensed to produce maple syrup commercially in Maine now. Of these, about three-quarters, maybe 350 producers, including Jackson Mountain Farm in Temple, put in less than two thousand taps. Another fifty producers in organized and populated Maine put in from two thousand to fourteen thousand taps. The remaining fifty, or so, occupy the several unorganized townships in northern Somerset County, formerly known as the Maine Maple Sugar District. These fifty—all Maine licensed producers—account for about 90 percent of Maine's maple syrup and are producing more every year. Somerset County Maine—fifty producers—leads the nation's counties in maple syrup production.

In June, Maine's annual Maple Mania, a summertime gathering of American and Canadian maple producers, vendors, and manufacturers comes to Jackman, Maine, a lonesome hamlet sitting near Canada in remote northern Somerset County. It is the third such summer gathering to celebrate Maine sugaring since 2011 when Maple Mania first appeared in Farmington. The gala is hosted by the Maine Maple Producers Association and its chapters, Southern Maine Maple Sugarmakers Association and the Somerset County Sugarmakers Association. In Jackman, producers, vendors, and manufacturers will exchange ideas, technology, and money—a vendor exhibit is part of the gala—and tour a list of local saphouses. I go to Jackman. I need to know what's happening in Somerset County.

Jackman is the gateway to the once Maine Maple Sugar District, a collection of townships along the Canadian border where maple syrup has been produced by nearby Quebeckers for more than a century. Sugaring—as it has everywhere—has changed in Somerset County. In 1935, 197 sugar camps populated the forest, and Canadian drum producers produced fifty thousand gallons of maple syrup yearly, according to the Maine Forest Service, and carted it back into Quebec for processing and packaging. About fifty licensed Maine producers, some, I suspect, a consortium of the 1935 sugar camps, produce syrup there in 2013. About two hundred producers, vendors, packers, and processors fill Mike's Moose Crossing, a local roadhouse on U.S. Route 201 in Sandy Bay Township, for the weekend. "We have the whole place to ourselves; Mike's is full," Lyle Merrifield, president of MMPA tells me. I find a place to sleep back down the road a ways at the Jackman Hotel.

Next day, Friday, I forsake the hotel and go back to Mike's for breakfast and the bus tour. We are scheduled to stop at seven sites. Two buses will shuttle the two hundred of us to the region's saphouses all day, interrupted only for lunch at Mike's. The first stop is at Wheeler's Maple in Bald Mountain Township.

Paul and Patti Wheeler came to the Sugar District in 2008. They built a saphouse in Bald Mountain Township on land owned and leased by Hilton Timberlands, and by 2010 they had put up a tubing network fit for twenty thousand tapholes. In 2013 they have thirty thousand in place and "thousands more are available," Paul says. He starts tapping the thirty thousand in January and finishes in March when he turns on the vacuum—four 10 hp liquid ring vacuum pumps—and leaves it on. He pumps his sap—3.2° Brix this year—to four five-thousand-gallon storage tanks at the Bald Mountain saphouse.

Two ROs reduce the sap—increase the concentration of sugar—to 20° Brix. A six-foot-by-eighteen-foot oil-fired evaporator boils the concentrate about a minute, while air is injected into both back and front pans, and produces 125 gallons of syrup per hour. "I make all light amber syrup," Wheeler tells us. He also tells us he made 350 drums—fourteen thousand gallons—of maple syrup in 2013 and sold it to one customer, the U.S. Organic Trade Association in Brattleboro, Vermont. The Wheelers are typical of sugarbush development in the former Maine Maple Sugar District, big, efficient, high quality. And he tells us he doesn't clean the tubing at the end of the season.

The bus takes us to Moose River Sugar Camp in Moose River, Maine, an organized Maine township of a bit more than two hundred people. Settled in 1820, Moose River's history is as a waypoint on the cattle drive from Boston to Quebec. Dale and Julie Forrester, owners of Moose River Sugar camp, came here ten years ago from Colewater, Michigan, and built a plastic tubing sap-gathering network for twenty thousand tapholes on land leased from Christian Camps and Conferences. Three pumping stations pump sap two miles uphill to the saphouse. Forrester says he uses polycarbonate spouts without the check valve and applies 25 inHg of vacuum. Sap is reduced by reverse osmosis to 12° Brix before boiling it off at a rate of fifty-five gallons of maple syrup per hour. From concentrate to syrup it takes about a minute of evaporator boiling time. We—the tour group—also learn that expansion is ongoing at Forrester's. His goal is thirty thousand tapholes and four pumping stations.

Forrester also imports sap from his neighbor, Kurt Sawyer, who does not have a saphouse and pumps his sap from five thousand tapholes on Boundary Bald Mountain to Moose River Sugar Camp. Sawyer uses check-valve spout adapters and limits tapholes to three per single tubing line. His vacuum—25 inHg—runs continuously as well. Sawyer pumps his sap to Forrester for a share of the syrup—60 percent—and continues to put in more taps. He tells us he plans a saphouse in a year or two, and expansion of his bush to twenty thousand tapholes. He also tells us he doesn't clean his tubing following the season, seemingly another common characteristic—peculiarity—of big producers in the former sugar district.

Joel Cloutier and Lisa Tanguay purchased the former Begin Sugarhouse—originally Libby's—in Sandy Bay Township in 2010. They started with twelve thousand tapholes. The following year, 2011, they shared the cost of a new bridge across the nearby Penobscot River with landowner Hilton Timberlands, and expanded. Cloutier-Tanguay now drills close to twenty thousand tapholes. Two pumping stations push sap overland, underground, and across the bridge to storage at their saphouse. Sap from the twenty thousand tapholes is processed through an RO and an outsized evaporator into about nine thousand gallons of maple syrup. Continuous expansion, Cloutier tells us, will eventually take them to forty thousand tapholes. At the end of Cloutier's presentation, he offers a taste of the maple syrup he produced in 2013. Inexperienced at tasting maple syrup boiled less than a minute—flash boiling—I sense it to be somewhat flat. The nice lady next to me doesn't think so. "Wonderful, isn't it?" she remarks. I smile.

These are all new folks the tour is taking us to. They've come into being since the start of the third millennium. Gone are the sugar camps of the 1920s and 1930s. In their place is modern sugaring. High-pressure, high-volume vacuum pumps, two-mile pipelines, sap-concentrating ROs, and outsized, high production, enhanced evaporators that produce more than one hundred gallons of maple syrup in an hour, have replaced the sap-shacks, two-horse teams, sap tubs, and stacks of split logs that fed a four-foot-by-twelve-foot drop-flue evaporator. Producers now burn barely a quart of fuel oil to produce a gallon of maple syrup.

Sugaring here in the Sugar District bears only a faint similarity to Orchard Hill in Temple. It's big sugaring. Each producer puts in mega-thousand taps. And the boiling rigs in the huge saphouses hide the boiling sap. Sap is unseen by human eyes and untouched by human hands from the tree to the draw-off, where it emerges as maple syrup. Our tour guides hold a cell phone in one hand and a clipboard in the other, monitoring what is going on in their sugarbushes—even in June.

We travel next to Vincent Guarino's Frontier Maple Sugarworks in Sandy Bay Township. Guarino taps trees on public land, two hundred acres of land leased by the State of Maine to the highest bidder. We stand in a gravel pit in the woods alongside U.S. Route 201 and listen to Guarino, who is standing on a good-sized log, tell us what he does. I see a bit of construction in progress; a six-foot-by-six-foot storage shack rises in the background. But no saphouse, no syrup, no evidence of any sap: sugar maples everywhere.

Guarino speaks. He won the lease in competitive bidding in 2011, started tapping in 2012. Put in a one-and-one-half-inch diameter wet line "up into the woods," he says. Drilled 2,600 tapholes. Guarino's lease permits seventy tapholes per acre—fourteen thousand tapholes in all. He sells his sap—delivers it—to Arnold Farm Sugarhouse across U.S. Route 201. He plans, he tells us, to relocate his pumping station, construct a saphouse, "and make my own syrup next year. Then I'll see where I am."

A man in the crowd asks Guarino, "Why do you make maple syrup?"

Guarino answers, "Why does anyone make maple syrup?" The bus moves on.

Gary and Heather Merrill, owners of Ledge Hill Farm in Cornville, Maine, came to Bald Mountain Township in 2009 and straight away put in an adjunct endeavor of 1,200 tapholes on land leased from Hilton Timberlands. Currently, they put in fifteen thousand taps and produce about 6,300 gallons of maple syrup. Their boiling rig includes a Steam-Away heat exchanger—free evaporation, Gary calls it—and boils off 21° Brix sap at the rate of nearly one hundred gallons of syrup per hour. Merrill tells us that air injection into the boiling pans "stirs up the sugar sand and eases the filtering." Air also, it is well known, lightens the syrup.

They sell syrup bulk in five-gallon plastic containers and fifty-five-gallon steel drums; retail it in five sizes of consumer plastic and a myriad of designer glass. The Merrills also make sugar and candy. They project their endeavor to reach fifty thousand tapholes in Bald Mountain Township "in just a few short years."

Andre Carrier, Carrier Sugarhouse, leases taps on both sides of U.S. Route 201. A Quebecker, Carrier speaks only French. Eric Ellis, vice president of MMPA and host of the Maple Mania celebration, translates. Carrier came here in 2009. Put in five thousand taps on leased land in Sandy Bay Township, the west side of U.S. Route 201. He currently puts in seventeen thousand, divided unequally between Sandy Bay Township and Moose River. He starts tapping January 1, filters his sap through a seven-post RO to 20° Brix, and produces 125 drums, 6,250 gallons, of pure Maine maple syrup. "The work is in the woods," Ellis translates, "and so is the money." Expansion is ongoing. Carrier is aiming for forty thousand tapholes and three pumping stations.

Producers here in Somerset County have goals. No one is big enough, yet. The size of the available resource—number of sugar maples—is unknown. Unlike Jackson Mountain Farm's goal of a thousand tapholes on Orchard Hill in Temple, the popular number here is forty thousand, and ranges up to eighty. I don't know whether it's a makeable goal in every case, but everyone we've listened to under forty thousand tapholes is aiming for that number, or higher. Rodney Boyington, a University of Maine graduate in civil engineering and now a successful contractor in Southern Maine, has acquired a lease here but has not drilled a hole in a tree yet. He's aiming to drill fifty thousand annually. Claude Rodriguez is already there—and more.

Arnold Farm Sugarhouse in Sandy Bay Township is owned and operated by Claude and Francois Rodriguez. It's an example of sugaring as big as it gets. In 1999, Rodriguez, a Quebecker and electrical engineer, and his son, Francois, both intrigued with the potential in the booming sugaring business, purchased fourteen acres of land in Sandy Bay Township and leased tapping rights on three thousand acres of adjacent Northern Mixed Hardwood Forest—predominantly sugar maples—from Hilton Timberlands. They constructed a Walmart-sized saphouse, modified it to include living space, and put up a pole line—168 utility poles—connecting the saphouse to the nearest electricity, seven miles away in Quebec, Canada. By the spring of 2000 Claude and Francois had established a twenty-thousand-taphole sugarbush on the three thousand leased acres and installed an underground piping network to pump sap to the saphouse.

Year after year following the spring of 2000, Claude and Francois expanded their sugarbush. In 2013, the Rodriguezes have reached fifty thousand tapholes and have reset the goal to eighty thousand. They have also added four thousand square feet to their original saphouse, installed upscale reverse osmosis—thirty-six membranes—and increased their syrup production rate to three drums—120 gallons—per hour. Five pumping stations from as far as 2.5 miles away push the sap to the saphouse.

Sap is concentrated by the two eighteen-membrane ROs to 20° Brix. The concentrate is boiled in a six-foot-by-eighteen-foot CDL Tornado oil-fired evaporator that features an add-on heat exchanger—what CDL calls a steam pan—that uses waste steam to bring the incoming sap to boiling temperature, similar to the Leader company's patented Steam-Away. Claude Rodriguez, who demonstrates to the Mania crowd his control over the five pumping stations by fingering an Apple iPad in his saphouse: turning the remote pumps on, measuring the present rate of sap flow—zero in this case—and then turning the pumps off. He claims to use only thirty-five gallons of fuel oil to boil off 125 gallons of syrup in an hour on the Tornado, less than 0.3 gallons of fuel per gallon of maple syrup. The Rodriguezes' operation, though one of the very largest in Maine, is typical of the present expansion goals of the fifty-some producers in the once-called Maine Maple Sugar District.

When four o'clock comes, we have stopped seven times, listened to seven producers hype their systems, tasted syrup, eaten ice cream, and in my case made notes. The bus takes us back to Mike's in Moose River where the vendor exhibit is in session and the predinner bar is open. I note the presence of Bruce Gillilan, head of the Leader Evaporator Company, and his Maine distributors Gwen Kinney, Kinney Maple Supplies in Knox, and Kevin Brannen, Spring Break Maple in Smyrna.

Gillilan and I chat briefly. He recalls when I was a distributor for Leader and tells me Leader has developed a new filter press, clear plastic frames—up to fifteen—that don't absorb heat and that keep the syrup hot during filtering. "My press," I tell him, "is a five-inch aluminum with a manual pump, so small it's not made anymore. And my batches are so small the syrup doesn't have time to cool."

Gillilan grins but doesn't say anything.

"I'll keep what I have a while longer," I say. "Keeps me in shape."

"But you can see the syrup going through a clear plastic press and know when the frames are full," he argues. "You won't blow out the bladder."

CDL, a Canadian-founded maple sugaring equipment manufacturer with a U.S. presence in St. Albans, Vermont, is also exhibiting here. CDL dealers here from Maine are Lyle and Jo Ann Merrifield, Merrifield Farms in Gorham, and Miguel Ibarguen, Bowley Brook Maple in Weld. But the featured vendor here at Mike's Moose Crossing is Sirocco, the only proven wood pellet evaporator on the market, so the sign says. I take a rack card for Joe.

I talk to Joe and Adele Suga, Vassalboro dealers for Dominion and Grimm, Lapierre, and Marcland equipment manufacturers. Lapierre is featuring the Lapierre Hurricane, a solid wood gasification evaporator. I talk to Joe about it. "Converts to wood pellets in a snap," he says. "It's similar to Ibarguen's Intens-O-Fire, efficient and versatile."

Efficiency is a key word at this exhibit, I notice, but competition for container sales is frantic. Dealers here, both United States and Canadian, are hyping consumer sizes in plastic, metal, and glass, and bulk sizes in plastic and stainless steel. Producers are talking feverously to dealers for next year's best prices. If a producer isn't able to find what he wants here at Mike's, or what he wants to know, he doesn't need it. Producers looking for a deal have until dinnertime and all day tomorrow to come up with one. I'm not looking for containers. I use Kinney's Maple Supplies in Knox for consumer-size containers in both Bacon plastic and Sugar Hill XL plastic. I use the Sugar Hill XL plastic for light and medium amber syrups and the Bacon plastic, which is less costly but doesn't hold the grade longer than four months, for dark and extra dark amber. I'm not quite as well fixed on my current boiling equipment, however, having committed Jackson Mountain Farm to an energy-use consultant. So I shy away from the evaporation apparatus and look for a dinner table that includes Gillilan.

Gillilan has offered good advice to me in the past. Twice recently, his advice has rewarded me handsomely. "Your tubing layout," he told me during a visit to Orchard Hill in 2011, "needs to be redone; the sap has to work too hard to get to your storage tank." And earlier, his demonstration of the value of the controversial check-valve adapter at an MMPA meeting in Augusta in January resulted in many skeptics, including me, trying it. And he was right. So at the dinner table in Jackman I ask him, "What's new?"

"You're using too much fuel," he says with a grin, like he's talked to my consultant already.

"But four gallons is pretty normal for a small producer," I say, "especially with 2 percent sap and no boiling enhancements."

"You could do better," he says, "and the enhancements will pay for themselves."

Gillilan is telling me like it is. I know about his Steam-Away, a heat exchanger that is capturing the minds of every commercial producer in Maine. It heats incoming sap to near the boiling point and dispenses distilled hot water at the same time. "But I need more sap to justify the price you have on it," I contend. Again, he tells me what I already know.

"Put in more taps, he says, and shorten your tubing lines, maximum five taps on a line." Following dinner I find the lounge at the Jackman Hotel and think about what Bruce has told me. Why not, I muse? Why not limit it to less than five tapholes per line? I've heard some progressives limit tapholes per line to three.

Saturday morning I pick out a technical session. First one starts at 9:00, a how-to session on judging maple contests. I've run into a bumpy road lately with contests. I've lost points for erratic density and off-flavor. I've been disqualified for alleged grading errors and made mistakes preparing—that is, tampering with—my sample. I'm in a learning phase again. So I go to the judging session.

The workshop is held at the Forest Hill School in Jackman. Professor Kathryn Hopkins leads the session. She tells us it will be interactive, participative schooling. We—an audience of producers—will judge syrup samples, she says, find the best taste, determine the winner. The entries are samples submitted by producers attending the Mania, many of them perhaps producers we visited yesterday. She divides the class into four groups, one group for each syrup grade. My group—six of us—will judge the flavor of eight dark amber entries.

Hopkins, to get us started, describes acceptable taste. "The typical maple syrup," she tells us, "has a unique flavor that makes it sensitive to out-of-the-ordinary contaminates that might be present in the production stream." Flavor, she says, can be affected by geography, age of the sap, whether the tree has budded, type of defoamer, length of boil, and even foreign sources of off-flavor, such as chlorine, soap, paint, metal, and mustiness. Flavors, once acceptable—or tolerable—in small doses such as smoke, caramel, and buds, are now undesirable. Smoke, for example, was once a component of flavor so common as to be expected. Even caramelized syrup, the product of a lengthy boil, was once considered acceptable, perhaps even desirable. But now it's an off-flavor. And buddy syrup, a late-season syrup with a taste likened by at least one expert at Cornell University to that of a bitter Tootsie Roll, has a limited market. No longer acceptable for consumer packaging, buddy syrup can only be processed into useful food and tobacco flavoring. Importantly for us, we must find off-flavor absent in ribbon-winning maple syrup.

So what is left that sets one syrup's taste apart from another? We, the six amateur judges, discuss what we should find in a winning flavor. Most of us know that when sap is boiled into maple syrup the taste is always maple, but as the boil lengthens the taste strengthens. Darker-colored syrups take on a stronger, sharper maple flavor. Though taste is subjective, we know that dark amber syrup has its own distinctive taste of maple—stronger on the palate, savory, tangy, or zesty, but always maple with no distractions. That characteristic, we agree, is what we will search for—or taste for—in the eight contest samples.

The samples are identified one through eight, each in a separate tasting jar. We taste them in order and note the relative standing of each. I find no off-tastes. I do select four samples, however, that taste weak or shallow, different to me than the strong, deep flavor that identifies dark amber maple syrup. The scrawny taste, I suspect, comes out of a lack of lengthy boiling. The weak taste, though maple, is caused by flash boiling. The sap has been boiled for perhaps a minute. No producer with an RO boils 2 percent sap. ROs exist for the single purpose of increasing Brix and shortening boiling time. Our tour through the sugar district did not take us to a producer without an RO. No sap reaches the boiler here in Somerset County that has not been concentrated. Of the seven producers on the tour, six reduce their sap to 20° Brix, the other to 12° Brix.

In the schoolhouse I select four of the eight samples that I think rate another taste. The remaining four, in my judgment, lack the hefty taste of dark amber maple syrup. They taste blank, flat, ho-hum. We, the six amateur judges, all agree that we cannot detect any off-flavor. We agree they all taste maple. But there is controversy over which is ribbon-winning syrup. Some judges perceive the same differences that I do. Some don't. "The difference comes from lack of a lengthy boil," I say. "Much sap these days is in the boiling pans less than a minute, and I'm convinced that hearty-tasting syrup needs a longer boil than a minute. Nothing else here in the district is as contrary to the rest of the state as the boiling time. Certainly the terroir—climate, topography, and soil—is the same as downstate."

"But my sap is filtered by an RO, and it doesn't taste like this," someone says.

"But concentrate at 8° Brix would boil as long as ten minutes," I reply. "Ten minutes may be enough to put some dark flavor into it."

This syrup, the syrup we've just tasted, lacks any caramel taste, which is usually produced by a lengthy boil. Less-than-a-minute syrup lacks dark amber maple gusto, zest. I convince the judges to discard the four no-zest samples as a group, and we taste the four zesty samples a second time. We agree on the ribbon winners.

Syrup judging closes the 2013 Maple Mania for me. Though a tech session on the best way to set up a tubing system is still to come, I'm ahead of that. Jackson Mountain Farm has its own plan to revise its tubing network, a plan that has twice come from the instructor of the tech session, Bruce Gillilan. I leave for Temple to see Joe and get started.

Chapter Twenty-Eight

FULL OF HOPE

THE 2013 SEASON AT JACKSON MOUNTAIN FARM—PRODUCTION DOWN 40 percent—is disappointing. I suspect bacteria may have again found a way through our defenses and contaminated the tapholes. Or perhaps we don't actually have a flawless sap collection system—not yet. Perhaps I set the vacuum shutoff temperature too high and what sap remained in the lines as liquid crept back into the holes and hindered the flow. Whatever, we need a fix. I decide to set the shutoff switch four degrees lower. The lower setting will ensure that the vacuum pump will run until the ambient temperature drops below 28°F. All sap in the lines should surely be frozen by then.

I meet Joe at the saphouse. We talk about what's next. Joe's long-term goal, he tells me, is a thousand tapholes and two hundred gallons of maple syrup. I agree with his goal and am excited to help him achieve it. And I know that a sufficient number of sugar maples are only a bit farther up Orchard Hill. But if Gillilan's tubing layout plan will actually produce a quart of syrup per taphole, I reason, we won't have to go up there. "We can tap another three hundred farther up the mountain and reach the two hundred gallons that way," I tell Joe, "or we can give Gillilan's tubing layout a chance, revise our lines, and make the two hundred gallons right here without slogging up the mountain any farther. I'd like to first find out what Gillilan meant when he told me our tubing layout is outmoded, producing only about half what it can." Joe agrees that reconfiguring the existing tubing layout is the first priority.

We plan what we will do: install a new and larger mainline stretching about halfway up the bush; juxtapose a vacuum line with the mainline, a separate path for pulling air out of the tubing. As it stands now, both sap and air are transferred through the mainline. Additional sap, which we expect with the reconfigured tubing network, will likely overcome the capacity of our present three-quarter-inch mainline and interfere with vacuum flowing up the hill—actually air flowing down the hill—and thereby prevent vacuum from reaching the tapholes. We will connect the supplementary vacuum line, the dry line, directly to each lateral as it proceeds up the hill and deliver a full charge of vacuum to even the most distant taphole without interference from sap running down the mainline, essential for maximum negative pressure—suction—at the top.

We talk about boiling capacity and our ability to boil off the increase in sap yield with the rig we have now. Should we be successful in doubling our sap yield, I expect we will need more boiling capacity, perhaps as much as 50 or 75 percent more. Our options to increase it are several: acquire a larger evaporator, enhance our existing rig with a preheater or an air injection system, increase the sugar concentration in the sap with reverse osmosis, or simply boil long hours. Money comes into our talk. Making more syrup will cost more money, of course. But we intend to reduce the cost per gallon of syrup produced by producing more gallons per hour, and using less fuel in the same hour—more syrup, less cost. Gathering more sap from the existing tapholes and boiling it off more efficiently on the rig we own is likely our best option—if we can achieve it. But first we need to know more about the alternatives. This will require professional advice. We start with a consultant search.

The search takes us to Mark Iacocca and GDS Associates in Manchester, New Hampshire, a national multiservice consulting engineering firm with expertise in energy and efficiency. Joe applies to USDA for an agricultural grant, a grant that will pay for conducting an energy analysis of our collecting and boiling processes, for recommending an energy management plan, and for putting the recommendations in place. Iacocca is critical to our success. He will perform the energy audit, analyze the data, and prepare what GDS Associates calls an Agricultural Energy Plan. USDA reimbursement of energy improvements depends on the outcome of Iacocca's analysis, the recommendations in his Agricultural Energy Plan. His fee is $2,200 payable in advance.

Iacocca comes to the Orchard Hill saphouse in June 2013 wearing boon dockers on his feet and carrying a briefcase in one hand. He introduces himself as an engineer, looks around while he chats with Joe and me, and jots a note on a pad he pulls from a shirt pocket. He seems a sociable man, maybe midthirties. "Been to Maine before?" I ask.

"Yes," he says, "but only for saphouse audits." I get that he knows his job, and he goes about doing it. He opens the briefcase and takes out a sheaf of data, much of it compiled by me: amounts of syrup production, electric use, and fuel oil consumption in the saphouse during the past three years. He reviews the data briefly and then says, "What's happening here is not unusual. Four gallons of fuel oil is pretty much the norm to make a gallon of syrup out of 2° Brix sap."

"I assume you're going tell us how to fix that with the rig we have here," I say.

"What do you want to do?" he asks.

"Well, Joe and I have talked about burning wood. There's plenty of it out there," I answer, pointing out the window. "But there's no consensus on that."

He tells us that wood has a price no matter the source. And that wood is usually inefficient, in fact the most inefficient fuel of any. "I'll include wood in the analysis so you'll know what I mean," he answers. "But what you really need here is an RO."

An RO is the easy answer, I think. I see a lot of them in the saphouses I visit. I also hear about RO from producers. Producers laud reverse osmosis. But reverse osmosis has never interested me. It violates the culture; takes me away from the sugaring experience. "We're not looking for an RO," I tell Iacocca. "An RO must be protected from freezing. We can't keep an RO warm in here. An RO," I tell him, "is complicated. Has stacks to clean, filters to wash, and is expensive. We produce too little sap here for an RO to be cost effective. There's not enough payback with an RO."

"What would you like?" he asks again.

I tell him we'd like to produce two hundred gallons of maple syrup. "We're revising the plastic network right now to maximize sap yield from the tapholes we have, and we can expand up the hillside should we need more to make the two hundred, perhaps add another hundred tapholes. Joe and I think a steam pan would work here. We're a small producer, less than a thousand taps, in a rustic setting. We'd like to see your numbers work for Leader's Steam-Away heat exchanger." Iacocca takes more notes. He measures the size of the saphouse and the evaporator pans. He counts and determines the wattage of our light bulbs. He reads the nameplate on the vacuum pump and tries to find one on the oil burner. He writes all this information in his notebook. After an hour here he leaves.

Iacocca's report, what he calls an Agricultural Management Plan for Jackson Mountain Farm, comes later in the summer. His analysis appears to work for us—functionally, financially, and environmentally. He recommends that we preheat the incoming sap with steam by installing a heat exchanger—Leader's Steam-Away—over the existing flue pan. This steam pan will raise the temperature of incoming sap, which must flow through the heat exchanger to reach the flue pan, to about 195°F, Iacocca writes in his report, and increase the concentration of sugar in our 2° Brix sap, to 7° Brix, a bit more than I had anticipated. An energy efficiency comparison with an RO, which Iacocca insisted that he do, indicates that boiling efficiencies and energy savings are about the same with either apparatus. The total cost of the RO, however, including operating costs —electricity—is about twice that of the Steam-Away. His report also praises the Steam-Away for less greenhouse gas emissions and less air pollutants than an RO. Based on Iacocca's analysis, USDA awards us a grant sufficient to pay for the Steam-Away, about $9,000, and Joe orders it from the Leader Evaporator Company immediately. Delivery is scheduled for October 2015. In the meantime Joe and I will proceed with our new sap-gathering scheme.

The 2015 sugaring season produces a considerable increase in syrup production over the previous three years. Though we finish tapping on March 8, the weather continues seasonably cold, and the first run of sap doesn't come until March 25, three days after Maine Maple Sunday.

Following the open house, however, which sees about thirty-five visitors come to the saphouse in below freezing temperature to order maple syrup for pickup later, the sap loosens, and we produce sixteen batches of maple syrup over the next nineteen days. The last sap run comes April 12, seventeen days after the first run, one of the shortest seasons ever. But a remarkably consistent stretch of temperature fluctuation produces eighty gallons—one pint per taphole—of syrup. One pint of syrup per taphole has long been considered a normal crop for wooded sugarbushes producing 2° Brix sap. Though customarily a season takes up four or five weeks, we've done it here in seventeen days.

Level production of sap is unusual. In the past, I've never known what I'll find in the tank when I go to the saphouse. But this year, 2015, is the closest we've come to a consistent supply. The tank fills day after day. I observe two corrections in our process that may have caused level production over the seventeen days. First, Joe is able to plug air leaks in the tubing system sufficient to build the vacuum to a consistent 13 inHg. While this is a bit lower than the pump rating, the consistency keeps the sap flow steady. Second, adjusting the shutoff setting on the vacuum pump to 28°F keeps the pump running until there is no liquid left in the lines and no bacteria to contaminate the hole, also contributing to an even flow of sap. We did, however, sustain a less-than-maximum vacuum level of only 13 inHg. I reason that the moderate loss of vacuum comes not from the pump's inability to maintain its rated level of 16 inHg but from the convoluted and inefficient tubing disarrangement we have cobbled together over many years. Replacement of the tubing lines to a proven and hydraulically efficient system will result, I expect, in a quantum jump in sap yield. Joe and I plan to rearrange the network and improve the hydraulics on about half the hill this summer and fall. We should have about half our answer by the spring of 2016.

We start work on the changes as soon as the 2015 season is over. Using a plan I have created from Bruce Gillilan's twice-given advice, verified by observing plastic tubing layouts in Somerset County in 2013, we first take down the lower five hundred feet of existing three-quarter-inch plastic mainline. We put up, roughly along the same easterly—lower—property line, a one-inch line in its place. This will add sap-carrying capacity to the lower end of the mainline. But since the stream of sap through the one-inch mainline will likely block the orderly removal of air from the laterals and tubing, we add five hundred feet of a separate one-and-one-quarter-inch vacuum line parallel and a bit above the one-inch wet line, and plug its upper end. This line completes a new wet/dry mainline, which forms the spine of our plan. The dry line is connected to each lateral line directly, and a full vacuum will reach the tapholes without interference from sap coming down the wet line.

Next we install the new lateral lines. At approximately ninety-foot intervals along the wet line we connect three-quarter-inch lateral lines running at right angles uphill through the sugar maples to near the westerly property line. We do this six times, wiring the laterals onto new support wires and plugging the upper ends. We then connect the intercepted tubing lines to the laterals with an airtight saddle in five-taphole segments. We work at this project—Phase I—all summer and fall. In October we learn that delivery of our Steam-Away has been delayed a month. In December, the Steam-Away still absent, we finish Phase I, about four hundred tapholes, a tad more than half the bush, and wait for the arrival of the Steam-Away.

The Steam-Away, fabricated in Swanton, Vermont, for delivery promised September 2015, arrives at Orchard Hill Road on January 19, 2016. More than a foot of snow covers the ground in Temple. The old three by twelve Leader Special lies on pallets in the front of the saphouse, its flues filling up with the newly fallen snow. Jackson Mountain Farm is the first stop on a six-stop tour of Maine saphouses for Leader's delivery crew. The second stop is scheduled for Bacon Farm Maple Products in Sidney later today, the sixth and last at Spring Break Maple Farm in Smyrna Mills, likely later tonight—or tomorrow. Also in Leader's delivery truck is a one-year-old three-foot-by-twelve-foot Leader MAX flue evaporator—flue pan and front pan—that we have leased from Northeast Leasing Corporation, also in Swanton, Vermont, for three years with an option to buy for $1 at the end of the lease period.

Joe has assembled a crowd of locals to bear the new apparatuses into the saphouse. It's slow work. At eleven o'clock when the three crated, shiny, annealed, stainless steel evaporator pans are safely jammed into the crowded sapshack, the Leader truck pulls away on its long, circuitous route to Smyrna Mills.

Joe has six weeks of Temple winter before the first likely sap run, five weeks should the run come early. In that time, he must assemble the new rig on the old arch and attach it to our suddenly decrepit storage tank, all with only what meager help I and whomever he has recruited can give him. Ten days later Justin Dimuzio, his soon-to-be brother-in-law, comes to the saphouse with a concrete saw and adjusts the dimensions of the old arch to fit the new MAX flue pan. In another ten days Joe assembles a second lifting crew, one of whom is Bill, his father and one of the three founders of Jackson Mountain Farm, to place the Steam-Away atop the MAX flue pan. By February 13, the Steam-Away is firmly in place on the modified arch, and Joe has started tapping sugar maples. Four days later, Jeff Butler, a back-to-the-land maple producer from Dresden, Maine, comes to the saphouse and rescues the old Leader Special from the snowbank, the final act in the transformation of our old Leader Special into a MAX flue evaporator with a Steam-Away preheater. Joe shows up to help with the lift. While there, he tells me, "I'll have the taps in and be ready to boil in a week."

March 6. I turn on the vacuum pump in anticipation of a warm front predicted to arrive in the next twenty-four hours. The front comes on schedule and brings the first sap run with it, the run that will test our half-finished tubing renovation, as well as the new Steam-Away. Two days later, the temperature rises to 45°F for the first time in Temple since early November. A second sap run, a somewhat meager one, comes with it and lasts through a snowy night and another day. We fire up the MAX flue and Steam-Away on March 10, and boil off about five gallons of dark amber syrup, our first experience with the new rig. It takes us about an hour, and the boil is trouble-free.

The sap run lasts eight days—and most nights. We boil off syrup every day until March 19 when the temperature drops to 18°F, shutting down the flow. Following a cold weekend—11°F—oscillating tempera- tures come back to Temple for another week. Again, sap runs every day and most nights. We boil it off afternoons. On Maine Maple Sunday— March 27—we boil off a full tank, a rarity for the annual open house. On

March 31, the temperature in Temple reaches 63°F and sap runs through the night before it stops. I turn off the vacuum on April 3.

The last boil-off—April 1—brings the year's production up to 130 gallons, 60 percent above the previous year. Fuel use drops to 2.2 gallons of oil per gallon of syrup, a remarkable 45 percent decline from previous years—all of this the result of boiling efficiencies coming from the pairing of the Steam-Away with the MAX flue pan. It's a noteworthy year, yet one we've planned on. To reach our goal of two hundred gallons of syrup per year, I expect we'll need only to finish the tubing renovation and add taps to a few scattered and untapped sugar maples within the confines of the existing network.

Following the 2016 season and the success of the steam pan, Beth and I continue the tubing remake—what we call Phase II. We extend the dry line another two hundred feet and string two more three-quarter-inch lateral lines on wires out into the bush. We connect the tubing lines to the laterals in segments of three tapholes, rather than five, as we had done in Phase I. Joe works above us, applying the same configuration to the highest portion of the existing network, about 175 tapholes, where expansion, should it be necessary, will happen. Beth and I finish Phase II, something more than three hundred tapholes, before Thanksgiving.

We are full of hope. About two-thirds of the bush has endured the reconfiguration, and we anticipate a likewise increase in syrup production. Joe finishes the 2017 tapping on March 5. Though a bit later than customary, it's just in time for the return of winter to Temple, as an early March blast of arctic air drops the daytime temperature to the midtwenties. The freezeup lasts until March 20 when the cold gives way slightly to warmer air, presumably from Dixie, and we begin to see sap in the lines occasionally. By Maine Maple Sunday, March 26, we have packaged in various-sized containers about ten gallons of maple syrup. We open the saphouse at 11:00 a.m. and the ten gallons is gone in half an hour.

During the remaining days of March, we produce and package thirty-five gallons of syrup, considerably less than our normal pace and well short of filling our list of annual orders. I'm anxious, afraid that the season will be a bust. But the daily temperature, like a pendulum, keeps swinging, and the sap keeps coming. We boil sap virtually every day for the next two weeks and produce one hundred gallons of syrup in April, finishing on April 15 with no loss of sap flow to the pesky microbe. Continuous vacuum, I believe, is the straw that broke the back of the incessant *Pseudomonas geniculata*. We finish the year at about 145 gallons, about three-quarters of our two-hundred-gallon goal.

Chapter Twenty–Nine

CHAMPIONS

In 2017, Maine sugarmakers, after a remarkable thirty-year run in growth and production of maple syrup, reach 709,000 gallons of maple syrup produced, literally beyond the graph, a growth performance rarely achieved for any manufactured or agricultural product. In 1987, Maine producers boiled off five thousand gallons of maple syrup. Thirty years later annual production reaches nearly three-quarter million. This remarkable upsurge in production comes from technology: the introduction of plastic tubing gathering systems, the use of vacuum, the control of bacteria, and the creation of efficient evaporating processes.

Jackson Mountain Farm during its lifetime has likewise benefited from this same technology. Though we have reduced our tapholes from three thousand to seven hundred—75 percent—technology has kept us near our historic annual production, about two hundred gallons. In 1964, our first year, we produced 220 gallons, a number we expect to come close to in 2018 with only a quarter of three thousand tapholes. And we will make higher quality and less costly syrup doing it.

Has Maine reached its limit producing maple syrup? Some say it has; that Maine cannot sustain its current mega-percent annual growth. I am not one of the naysayers. "Look at the 2011 Maple Task Force Study Group report to the Maine legislature," I say.

In 2011 the 125th Maine Legislature resolved to study the potential for promotion and expansion of the Maine maple sugar industry—Resolve Chapter 48, LD 109. The commissioner of agriculture convened a task force of producers, small woodlot owners, farming and forest organizations, and the University of Maine Cooperative Extension Service. Chaired by Representative Russell Black, Wilton maple producer, the task force studied Maine's maple sugaring potential and its economic benefits, and submitted its report to the Maine Legislature in December 2011.

The task force found that 89 percent of Maine is forested, about the same as when Stephen Titcomb came to Farmington in 1781 and made the first pure Maine maple syrup. The task force also found thirty-eight million red and sugar maple trees ten inches or more in diameter growing in Maine. It found forty-one million potential tapholes, thirty-three million in just five counties: Aroostook, Piscataquis, Somerset, Franklin, and Oxford. It found 375,000 acres of hardwood timberland—perhaps four million tapholes—on public land. Maine has a vast resource for expanding its sugaring, as many as forty-five million potential taps. In 2016, Maine producers put in two million taps; Vermont, with half the trees, five million; New York, a dite more than two million.

"Maine has a lot of work to do should it decide to catch up with New York and Vermont," so says Professor Kathryn Hopkins, maple specialist with the University of Maine Cooperative Extension Service. But the visionary Hopkins, prompted by a reporter touting Maine Maple Sunday, also says, "Yes, we have the trees. I believe we can do it." She also thinks we should decide now whether to go ahead, get organized for the future, recruit young producers, and commit to the marketing. And she makes her own position clear when she says, "Maine can do anything it wants."

Hopkins is not the only visionary in Maine, however, when it comes to Maine sugaring. Governor Paul LePage is our biggest champion. He produced maple syrup as a youth in New Brunswick on his family's farm, and he now, as governor, pushes Maine sugaring whenever he gets a chance—and wherever he is. At the annual first tap ceremony on the Blaine House lawn in 2014, LePage hyped the growing maple industry this way: "Maple syrup is an industry Maine could be leading America in," he beamed. "We have the capacity to outperform Vermont." Pushed for more comment, he responded, "That's right. We could be a national leader. Not only could we compete with Vermont," he said, "we could compete with Quebec. We could surpass them easily—and we have the forest to do it."

And Jackson Mountain Farm? What about us? We own 1,500 tapholes and an equipment resource for producing four or five hundred gallons of maple syrup. Our near-term goal is to put in some eight hundred taps and produce two hundred gallons of syrup annually, about half what we think the hill will yield. We think we will achieve the near-term goal within a year or so, but to reach our full potential we will need to make a commitment that we haven't made yet.

Jackson Mountain

The sign is the same as the one on the old slidin' door.
But the barren, hard-packed earth is now a cement floor.
The old weathered board walls are needin' of wear
To once again prove that time has passed there.

The old door used to slide on a rusty steel track
When the pile of birch slats wasn't holdin' it back.
Speakin' of birch and luggin' and pilin',
There's two oil burners a waitin' to be firin'.

Time sure has changed that old sugarin' off shack
For instead of pails on the trees
There's a long, blue snake in the back.
It slithers from maple to maple and down into the tank.
I guess it sure beats fallin' with full pails
Down over the bank.

The faces are familiar what with Bill, Brud, and John.
But, like the old shack itself, some others have gone.

You can never turn back the clock or relive moments again,
But, we remember the days of Monty and Slim.

With all these changes some things remain the same;
The sap keeps on runnin' and they're boilin' again.
The trees are still quite majestic standing tall in the snow.
Jackson Mountain where did you go?

From *Treasures of the Heart*
by Chandler Woodcock

SOURCES

Costilow, R. N. and Sheneman, J. M. *Identification of Microorganisms from Maple Tree Tapholes.* Michigan State University. 1958.

The Forests of Maine. USDA Resource Bulletin NE-164. 2005.

Garrett, H. Duchacek, Morselli, M., Laing, F., Huyler, N., and Marvin, J. "Increasing the Efficiency of Maple Sap Evaporators with Heat Exchangers." United States Department of Agriculture Forest Service. 1977.

Gooley, Walter R. "Up North It's 'Sirop D'erable.'" *Down East.* 1976.

Heiligmann, R., Koelling, M., and Perkins, T. *North American Maple Syrup Producers Manual.* Second Edition. The Ohio State University. 2006.

Hopkins, Kathryn. *Bulletin #7038, Maple Syrup Quality Control Manual.* University of Maine Cooperative Extension. 2007.

King, W., and Morselli. M. F. "Bacterial Adhesion to Plastic Tubing Walls." *Maple Syrup Digest.* 1983 23 (3).

Lawrence, J., and Martin, R. *Sweet Maple.* Chapters Publishing Ltd. Shelburne, VT and *Vermont Life* magazine, Montpelier, VT. 1993.

Maple Sugar Maker's Guide. The Leader Evaporator Company. Burlington, VT. 1961.

Morselli, Mariafranca. "Effects of the Use of Paraformaldehyde Sterilizing Pellets on Sugar Maple Health: A Review." International Union of Forest Research Organizations XXth World Congress. 1995.

Nearing, Helen and Nearing, Scott. *The Maple Sugar Book.* Chelsea Green Publishing Company, White River Junction, VT. 2000.

Open House Tour. Farmington Historical Society. 1970.

Perkins, Timothy D. "Development and Testing of the Check-Valve Spout Adapter." *Maple Syrup Digest* 21A (3).

The Season of the Feast of Sugar. Lewiston Sun Journal magazine section. April 1915.

Stevens, Cindy. *Stephen Titcomb and the Settlement of the Sandy River Valley.* Farmington Historical Society.

Whynott, Douglas, *The Sugar Season.* De Capo Press. Boston, MA. 2014.

Williams, Nellie Titcomb. "Maple Syrup Produced in Franklin County since 1781," *The Franklin Journal* c. 1950.

Willits, C. O. *Maple Sirup Producers Manual.* United States Department of Agriculture. 1976.

Yetter, Luann. *Remembering Franklin County.* The History Press, Charleston, SC. 2009.

ABOUT THE AUTHOR

John Hodgkins lives in Yarmouth, Maine. A retired civil engineer and adjunct civil engineering professor, he and his late wife Beth have been boiling sap in the Maine woods for more than fifty years. A Maine maple producer since 1964, his maple syrup has earned numerous awards, including a 2011 Best of Show in Maine's statewide contest. He served two terms in the 1990s as president of the Maine Maple Producers Association. He still maintains ties to his native Temple and spends a few months there each year raising Christmas trees and producing maple syrup.